WALKING
LONDON

WALKING
LONDON
THE BEST OF THE CITY

Sara Calian

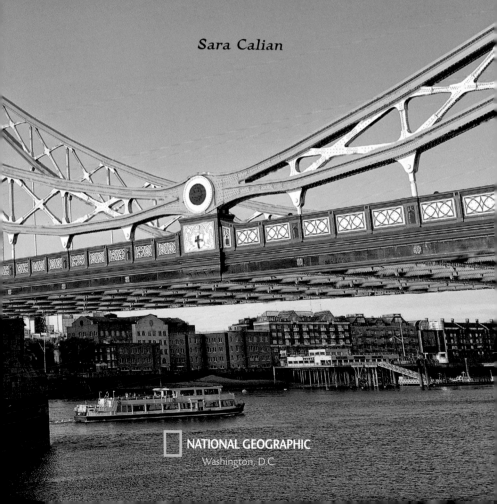

NATIONAL GEOGRAPHIC
Washington, D.C.

WALKING
LONDON

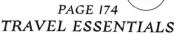

CONTENTS

PART **1**

PAGE 12
WHIRLWIND TOURS

PART **2**

PAGE 36
LONDON'S NEIGHBORHOODS

PART **3**

PAGE 174
TRAVEL ESSENTIALS

**Previous pages:
Tower Bridge;
left: The Lord
Mayor's Show;
above right: Chelsea
Pensioners at the
Royal Hospital
Chelsea; right:
Statue of Eros in
Piccadilly Circus**

Introduction

Samuel Johnson, the great British writer, once said that he who tires of London tires of life. I've never tired of the city, though it has frequently left me exhausted. Because—mostly—I walk it. I've done so since I was unleashed on its streets at age 14 in the '60s. It was the Beatles' London then. Jazzed. Experimental. Full of life. Pretty much as it is today, but with a different cultural idiom, revolutionary architecture, and draconian traffic restrictions. The one thing that endures: The best way to experience this great city is to hoof it.

Navigate a city on foot and you feel, intimately, its energy. You connect with the place. You engage face to face with its inhabitants. Neighborhoods become neighborly, and storefronts draw you close. You begin to sense its cadence—where its energy ebbs and flows. You smell the flowers, read the fine print on monuments, stumble across local celebrations, lounge on park lawns, eavesdrop on workaday conversations, succumb to a nightclub beat, randomly sample an early morning espresso, or simply sit and watch as life passes by in natural high-def. While cars and cyclists must hew to a mostly prescribed route, walkers can ramble, divert, explore, linger, and follow their noses. Happenstance is the currency of the traveler who chooses to go step by step.

The Millennium Bridge links Tate Modern and the Globe Theatre on the south bank of the Thames to the City on the north side.

This book celebrates the art of the city walk. We invite you step out and navigate—we'll be with you stride for stride.

Keith Bellows

Former Editor-in-Chief, National Geographic Traveler *magazine*

Visiting London

London is one of the world's most culturally rich and dynamic cities, but with 8.8 million residents and 28 million visitors per year and an area of 607 square miles (1,600 sq km), it can be one of the most bewildering, even for seasoned travelers.

London in a Nutshell

From the time of the first Roman city (founded in A.D. 50) to today's modern metropolis, the River Thames has been at the heart of London. For centuries, it was the main highway for Londoners, and a boat trip or a walk along its pedestrianized South Bank still provides a great to way to understand the city. The Tower of London, St. Paul's Cathedral, Westminster's Houses of Parliament, and Tate Britain are all on the north bank, while a string of cultural institutions (the Globe Theatre, Tate Modern, and the South Bank arts complex) line the revitalized south side.

Navigating London

London's layout can be confusing— some streets twist and turn to a

London Day-by-Day

Monday Most sites are open except for Sir John Soane's Museum, Whitechapel Gallery, and Apsley House.

Tuesday Most sites are open except for Sir John Soane's Museum and Apsley House. The British Library is open until 8 p.m.

Wednesday All sites open. The British Library is open until 8 p.m.

Thursday All sites open. The British Library is open late (until 8 p.m.), as is Whitechapel Gallery (until 9 p.m.).

Friday Most galleries are open late, including the British Museum (until 8:30 p.m.), the National Gallery and National Portrait Gallery (until 9 p.m.), the Victoria and Albert Museum, Tate Modern, and the Royal Academy (until 10 p.m.). Spitalfields and Borough markets are open.

Saturday Museums and galleries are open, but the Old Bailey and the Houses of Parliament are closed. Tate Modern is open until 10 p.m. Portobello, Camden Lock, and Borough markets are all open.

Sunday Most museums and galleries are open, but the Old Bailey, and the Houses of Parliament are closed. Westminster Abbey and St. Paul's are open to worshipers only. Some theaters are open, including the Globe and National Theatres. Many shops are open but large stores can only trade for six hours between 10 a.m. and 6 p.m.

Two of London's most famous icons are outlined against a rare blue sky—the city's reputation for changeable weather is justified, so do pack an umbrella and raincoat.

bewildering degree, and many look similar to each other—but there are some tricks to navigating this enormous city on foot.

Helpful signs across the city present two maps of the local area, complete with street layout and landmarks. The first map shows what lies within a five-minute walking circle from that point; the second, a 15-minute walking circle. Underground stations also have local maps, often posted near the exit.

Don't rely on the river for orientation. Although most of central London is on the north side of the Thames, the river twists and turns so much that it is not reliable for direction. If you are looking across the Thames at Westminster, for example, you are in fact looking east, not south.

Crossing the Road

Jaywalking is not an offense in the U.K., and pedestrians are free to use their own judgment when crossing the street. Vehicles drive on the left side of the road, so you need to look to your right first before crossing—except when you are on a one-way street. And watch out particularly for cyclists because they hug the curbside, travel silently, and often ignore traffic signals.

Using This Guide

Each tour—which might be only a walk, or might take advantage of the city's public transportation as well—is plotted on a map and has been planned to take into account opening hours and the times of day when sites are less crowded. Many end near restaurants, theaters, or lively night spots for evening activities.

Whirlwind Tours

Whirlwind Tours are for people who have only a day or a weekend to spend in the city and want to be sure that they see the best of the best. Choose your tour based on your time and interests: One Day; Weekend (Day 1 & Day 2); For Fun; and With Kids (Day 1 & Day 2).

Tips For the Day and Weekend Tours, a Tips spread following the itinerary map provides insider information on detours from the key sites, extra places to see, nearby cafés and restaurants, and ideas for adapting the tours to suit your interests.

Site Descriptions For the For Fun and With Kids Tours, key sites spreads following the maps provide descriptions of all the sites and practical information for visitors.

Neighborhood Tours

The nine neighborhood tours each begin with an introduction, followed by an itinerary map highlighting the key sites that make up the tour and detailed key sites descriptions. Each tour is followed by an "in-depth" spread showcasing one major site along the route, a "distinctly" London spread providing background information on a quintessential element of that neighborhood, and a "best of" spread that groups sites thematically.

Itinerary Map A map of the neighborhood shows the locations of the key sites, Tube stations, and main streets.

Captions These briefly describe the key sites and give instructions on finding the next site on the tour. Page references direct you to full descriptions of the key sites on the following pages.

Route Dotted lines link the key sites.

Good Eats Refer to these lists for a selection of cafés and restaurants along the tour.

Key Sites Descriptions Following the order of the tour, these provide a detailed description and highlights for each site, plus address, phone number, days closed, entrance fee, nearest Tube station, and website.

Price Ranges for Key Sites

£	under £3
££	£3–£7
£££	£7–£12
££££	£12–£15
£££££	over £15

Price Ranges for Good Eats (for one person, excluding drinks)

£	under £12
££	£12–£20
£££	£20–£30
££££	£30–£50
£££££	over £50

PART 1

Whirlwind Tours

London in a Day

Get an overview of London's sights with this packed one-day tour.

❼ National Gallery (see pp. 92–93) **Explore the wonders of one of the world's greatest art collections. If you have time for just one painting, make it Vincent van Gogh's "Sunflowers."**

❶ Buckingham Palace (see p. 58) **Gaze up at the famous balcony where the royal family waves to the crowds on historic occasions. From the palace, the monarch's London residence since 1837, stroll through St. James's Park to Parliament Square.**

❷ Westminster Abbey (see pp. 64–65) **See the soaring Gothic arches of the great church, where 38 monarchs have been crowned. Turn right out of the abbey onto Parliament Square.**

**LONDON IN A DAY   DISTANCE: 6.5 MILES (10.4 KM)
TIME: APPROX. 8 HOURS   TUBE START: HYDE PARK CORNER**

6 St. Paul's Cathedral
(see pp. 48–49) **Climb 528 steps, past the Whispering Gallery, for a panoramic view of London. Catch a No. 15 heritage bus west toward Trafalgar Square.**

5 Tower Bridge (see pp. 162–163) **Visit the Victorian engine rooms to admire the gleaming machinery. Cross to the south bank of the river and follow the Thames Path west to the Millennium Bridge, then cross north for St. Paul's Cathedral.**

4 Tower of London (see pp. 168–169) **Yeoman Warders and the Crown Jewels are just some of the sights in this well-preserved royal fortress, founded by King William the Conqueror in 1066. Walk up the steps leading to Tower Bridge Approach.**

3 Houses of Parliament
(see pp. 50–59) **Big Ben's clock tower is an unmistakable landmark at the northern end of this Victorian Gothic masterpiece. Step down to Westminster Pier for the river taxi going east.**

Tips

These are the best of the best London sights. All are described elsewhere in the book—just follow the cross-references for more detailed information. The tips here provide advice on visiting these major sights when you have limited time. They also include additional sights nearby and places to eat.

❶ Buckingham Palace (see p. 58) If you want to know more about the bearskin-hat-wearing guards, head to the ■ **GUARDS MUSEUM** (*Wellington Barracks, Birdcage Walk, SW1, tel 020 7414 3271, closed public holidays and for other events, ££, theguardsmuseum .com*), which has artifacts from the five regiments that guard the palace.

City Hall, home to the London Assembly, was designed by architect Norman Foster.

❷ Westminster Abbey (see pp. 64–65) After exploring the abbey, visit ■ **THE VICTORIA TOWER GARDENS** (*Abingdon St., SW1*), adjacent to the Houses of Parliament. It's a peaceful park by the river that includes the ■ **BUXTON MEMORIAL FOUNTAIN**, which celebrates the emancipation of slaves in the British Empire in 1834.

❸ Houses of Parliament (see pp. 58–59) Parliament's quarter bells ring every 15 minutes, but ■ **BIG BEN** only chimes on the hour— but won't do so until 2021, due to repairs. A quick alternative to a tour around Parliament is the 700-year-old ■ **JEWEL TOWER** (*Abingdon St., SW1, tel 020 7222 2219, closed Jan.1, Dec. 24–26, weekdays Nov.–Mar., ££, english -heritage.org.uk*), which used to store royal jewels and now has displays on the history of Parliament. The fastest way to travel on the river is to use the

■ **THAMES CLIPPERS** river taxis (see p. 30). For a more leisurely option, take any one of several tour boats. These have their own guides, who bring the Thames to life with interesting facts and tales from the river's past.

❹ **Tower of London** (see pp. 168–169) Expect hour-long lines to get into the Tower of London. If you don't have time to wait, visit ■ **ALL HALLOWS BY THE TOWER** (*Byward St., EC3, tel 020 7481 2928, ahbtt.org.uk*), a Saxon church dating to A.D. 675. Sixth U.S. president John Quincy Adams was married here in 1797. Check out a nearby original section of the ■ **LONDON WALL** just outside Tower Hill tube station. Dating from around A.D 225, the 35-foot-high (10.7 m) wall defined the city's boundaries for more than a thousand years. If your feet are feeling tired, ■ **TRINITY SQUARE**, just north of the Tower, is a good place for a rest. The square was the site of most of London's public executions. It has a memorial to sailors lost during the two World Wars.

❺ **Tower Bridge** (see pp. 162–163) ■ **ST. KATHARINE DOCKS**, just east of Tower Bridge, has plenty of cafés and restaurants, making it a great place for lunch. In summer, you can enjoy free films, plays, and musical performances

CUSTOMIZING **YOUR DAY**

If you want to squeeze some shopping into your day, the One New Change shopping center *(One New Change, EC4, www.onenewchange.com)*, to the east of St. Paul's Cathedral, has fashion stores and jewelry and gift shops. Or you could get off the No. 15 bus on the Strand and walk through to the shops in Covent Garden (see p. 102).

at ■ **THE SCOOP**, a 1,000-seat outdoor amphitheater on the bridge's south side.

❻ **St. Paul's Cathedral** (see pp. 48–49) After touring the cathedral, head to nearby ■ **ST. BARTHOLOMEW'S HOSPITAL** (*West Smithfield, EC1, tel 020 7377 7000, bartshealth.nhs.uk/st-bartholomews*). Founded in 1123, it's Britain's oldest hospital, though most of the current building dates from the 18th century. Look for the plaque commemorating the death of Scottish hero William Wallace (aka Braveheart), who was executed near here in 1305.

❼ **National Gallery** (see pp. 92–93) After gazing at paintings by artists such as Paul Cézanne, Claude Monet, and Vincent van Gogh, dine in the gallery's ■ **NATIONAL CAFÉ** (see p. 140), which remains open even after the gallery has closed.

WHIRLWIND TOURS

London in a Weekend

*Spend your first day touring museums and palaces,
and enjoying exquisite shopping and wonderful views.*

REGENT'S
PARK

Madame Tussauds
Regent's Park
Great Portland Street

Marylebone Station
Baker St.

Marylebone

ROAD

PARK CRES

PORTLAND PL

MARYLEBONE

Edgware Road

GLOUCESTER

BAKER STREET

WIGMORE STREET

OXFORD

1 Madame Tussauds
(see p. 22) For nearly
200 years, wax models
have enthralled, shocked,
and at times appalled
visitors. Take the Tube to
Knightsbridge.

Marble
Arch

Bond
Street

PARK LANE

PARK LANE

MAYFAIR

2 Harrods (see
pp. 146–147) London's
most famous store has
a food court sumptuous
enough to satisfy any
palate. Walk west on
Brompton Road.

**HYDE
PARK**

The Serpentine

PICCADILLY
Green
Park
**GREEN
PARK**

KENSINGTON GORE

KENSINGTON RD.

KNIGHTSBRIDGE

Hyde Park
Corner

**Buckingham
Palace** 4

EXHIBITION RD.

KNIGHTSBRIDGE

Victoria and
Albert
Museum

Knightsbridge
Harrods 2

BELGRAVE
SQUARE

BELGRAVIA

Science
Museum

Natural History Museum
Hampton
& Kew

CROMWELL ROAD

Gloucester
Road

THURLOE PL

BROMPTON ROAD

South
Kensington

SLOANE STREET

BROMPTON

EATON SQ.

Sloane
Square

Victoria
Coach
Station

Victoria
**Victoria
Station**

3 Natural History Museum
(see pp. 136–137) Be awed by the
size of a blue whale, scared by the
teeth of a *T. rex*, or fascinated by a
stuffed polar bear. Take the Tube
to St. James's Park.

4 Buckingham Palace (see
p. 58) As well as admiring the
palace, check out the marble
memorial to Queen Victoria out
front. Walk through St. James's
Park, then south on Storey's Gate.

**LONDON IN A WEEKEND, DAY 1   DISTANCE: 6 MILES (9.5 KM)
TIME: APPROX. 7.5 HOURS   TUBE START: BAKER STREET**

8 Trafalgar Square (see p. 88) London's favorite public space, used for rallies and celebrations, is also full of public art such as a 170-foot-high (52 m) memorial to Admiral Lord Nelson, who defeated the combined French and Spanish fleets off Cape Trafalgar in 1805.

7 London Eye (see p. 74) Admire the view from London's 40-story-high (135 m) observation wheel. Cross the Golden Jubilee Footbridge, which flanks Hungerford Bridge, and walk west on Northumberland Avenue.

6 Houses of Parliament (see pp. 58–59) Although Big Ben, cast in 1858 at the Whitechapel Bell Foundry (which also cast the Liberty Bell in Philadelphia), is under repair until 2021, the magnificent Palace of Westminster building can be toured by booking in advance. Cross Westminster Bridge and take the steps to the London Eye.

5 Westminster Abbey (see pp. 64–65) Visit the royal family's most important church, where Prince William and Kate Middleton were married. Cross over Abingdon Street.

London in a Weekend

*Spend your second day visiting a
medieval castle, a baroque cathedral, a graceful bridge,
and a Victorian market.*

❶ Shakespeare's Globe (see p. 76) **Start the day with a
tour of the reconstructed Globe Theatre, built on the site
where William Shakespeare's plays were performed more
than 400 years ago. Head north across the Millennium
Bridge to St. Paul's Cathedral.**

❻ Tate Modern (see
pp. 78–79) **End the day
with a quick look around
the Turbine Hall—one of
London's largest gallery
spaces, which hosts
specially commissioned
exhibitions from
contemporary artists.**

Chancery
Lane
HIGH HOLBORN

ALDWYCH   FLEET

Temple

EMBANKMENT

VICTORIA   WATERLOO BRIDGE   *Thames*

GOLDEN
JUBILEE BR.

Waterloo
Waterloo
Station

WESTMINSTER BR.   WESTMINSTER   Lambeth
North

LAMBETH PALACE RD.

LAMBETH   ROAD

LAMBETH

**LONDON IN A WEEKEND, DAY 2   DISTANCE: 3.5 MILES (5.5 KM)
TIME: APPROX. 8 HOURS   TUBE START: MANSION HOUSE**

② **St. Paul's Cathedral** (see pp. 48–49) Explore London's largest and most breathtaking church. Walk east along Cheapside and Threadneedle Street, then north on Bishopsgate.

③ **Old Spitalfields Market** Enjoy lunch at one of this Victorian market's many eateries, before browsing the shops and stalls for the perfect gift or souvenir. Walk south on Commercial Street and then Mansell Street.

④ **Tower of London** (see pp. 168–169) London's 11th-century castle has something for everyone—historic armor, the Crown Jewels, and grisly stories from the tower's past. Walk up the steps to Tower Bridge Approach.

⑤ **Tower Bridge** (see pp. 162–163) A combination of Victorian engineering excellence and architectural splendor makes this one of the world's most memorable bridges. Cross to the river's south bank, and walk west along the Thames Path.

Tips

These major London sights can be seen in two days. Refer to the cross-references for detailed information elsewhere in the book. There's also information here on detours to nearby sights, on local cafés and restaurants, and suggestions for customizing the tour to suit your own interests.

DAY 1

❶ Madame Tussauds If it's a sunny day, walk south on Baker Street and west on Oxford Street to Marble Arch and continue south through ▪ HYDE PARK (see p. 138), one of London's largest green spaces and a former royal hunting ground, to Harrods.

Londoners relax and picnic in Hyde Park.

❷ Harrods (see pp. 146–147) Eat ▪ BRUNCH here, either in one of the store's many restaurants or in the wonderfully varied food hall.

❸ Natural History Museum (see pp. 136–137) If the Natural History Museum doesn't pique your interest, the ▪ SCIENCE MUSEUM (see pp. 132–133) or the ▪ VICTORIA AND ALBERT MUSEUM (see pp. 130–131) are excellent alternatives.

❼ London Eye (see p. 74) After riding on the Eye, bibliophiles can make a detour along the river past the Royal Festival Hall (see p. 74) to the ▪ SOUTH BANK BOOK MARKET, an open-air market selling secondhand books (open until around 7 p.m.). A little farther east is the arty enclave of ▪ GABRIEL'S WHARF (*56 Upper Ground, SE1, southbanklondon.com*), with craft shops, galleries, cafés, a small sandy beach, and views of the river.

❽ Trafalgar Square (see p. 88)
Admire some of the sculpture on Trafalgar Square, including a statue of first U.S. president ■ **GEORGE WASHINGTON**, whose plinth in front of the National Gallery stands on earth imported from Virginia in honor of Washington's pledge to never set foot on British soil. Finish your day with dinner in the crypt of ■ **ST. MARTIN-IN-THE-FIELDS** (see p. 89) before attending a concert of baroque music in the church. Many of the concerts are held by candlelight.

DAY 2

❸ Old Spitalfields Market
(*105a Commercial St., E1, tel 020 7247 8556, oldspitalfieldsmarket.com*) If you can't find what you're looking for at the rejuvenated Victorian-era Spitalfields market, try nearby ■ **BRICK LANE** (see p. 83), whose Sunday market is a popular hunting ground for chic clothing and bric-a-brac.

❹ Tower of London (see pp. 168–169) You can walk around three sides of the Tower of London, getting a great view of the walls without having to go in. On the river side, you can see ■ **TRAITOR'S GATE**, ■ **TOWER BRIDGE**, and a display of historic cannon.

CUSTOMIZING **YOUR DAY**

With at least one night in London, why not check out some of Europe's best nightlife? Enjoy a performance at the Royal Opera House in Covent Garden (see pp. 102–103) or modern drama at the National Theatre (see p. 75), or visit a small rock club in Soho. For the latest events, see the *London Evening Standard*, a free daily newspaper, and *Time Out*, a free weekly magazine.

❺ Tower Bridge (see pp. 162–163)
■ **BUTLER'S WHARF** (see p. 77) on the south side of the bridge has good restaurants and is a fine place to stop for lunch. On the walk along the river, you can make a detour south to the ■ **OLD OPERATING THEATRE** (*9a St. Thomas St., SE1, closed Dec. 5–Jan. 5, ££, tel 020 7188 2679, oldoperatingtheatre. com*), a short way south of London Bridge. This purpose-built theater in a garret over a hospital's church dates back to 1822 and has displays covering the history of surgery and nursing.

❻ Tate Modern (see pp. 78–79)
Even if you are not interested in contemporary art, pop in to see the ■ **TURBINE HALL**, a massive open space running the length of the building and extending up to the roof. The bridge across the hall at first-floor level is a good viewpoint.

WHIRLWIND TOURS

London for Fun

After a busy day of outings and shopping, relax with an English afternoon tea before an evening at the theater.

WHIRLWIND TOURS

❸ **Regent Street Shopping** (see p. 26) More retail-therapy awaits behind the facades of architect John Nash's 19th-century thoroughfare. At the foot of Regent Street, walk south on Swallow Street and then west on Piccadilly.

❷ **Grays Antiques** (see p. 26) Pick up a souvenir from this eclectic selection of vintage objects. Head south on Davies Street, then east on Brook Street and Hanover Street to Regent Street.

❶ **Knightsbridge Shopping** (see pp. 26, 146–147, 156–157) Shopping at Harrods and snacking at its famous food hall are a must before tackling the designer stores nearby. Take the Tube to Bond Street.

LONDON FOR FUN   DISTANCE: 6.8 MILES (11 KM) TIME: APPROX. 8.5 HOURS   TUBE START: SOUTHWARK

Chancery Lane
HOLBORN
Farringdon
HOLBORN VIA
City
Thameslink
FLEET STREET
Temple
VICTORIA EMBANKMENT
Blackfriars Sta.
Blackfriars
BLACKFRIARS BRIDGE
Thames
NORTH
SOUTHWARK
STAMFORD ST.
Southwark
Waterloo
Waterloo Station
Lambeth North

❻ American Bar at the Savoy (see p. 27) Quaff well-earned drinks at one of London's best bars. The Savoy Theatre is next door.

❼ Savoy Theatre (see p. 27) Catch a musical in this delightfully decorated art deco building

❺ No. 15 Heritage Bus (see p. 27) Enjoy a ride on a classic 1960s Routemaster double-decker bus. Get off at The Savoy.

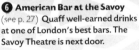

❹ Fortnum & Mason (see pp. 27, 69) Sipping afternoon tea while nibbling on clotted cream scones and listening to an excellent pianist is a quintessential British experience. Walk east to Regent Street and turn south to Pall Mall, then east to Trafalgar Square.

WHIRLWIND TOURS

Harrods' food hall has counters dedicated to tea, cheese, meat, bread, chocolate, and more.

Knightsbridge Shopping

1 Knightsbridge's streets hold London's top designer shops, including **Dior** *(31 Sloane St.)*, **Louis Vuitton** *(190–192 Sloane St.)*, **Chanel** *(135 Sloane St.)*, **Giorgio Armani** *(37–42 Sloane St.)*, **Prada** *(43–45 Sloane St.)*, and **Saint Laurent** *(170 Sloane St.)*. There are also some opulent department stores, such as **Harvey Nichols** (see p. 156) and **Harrods** (see pp. 146–147), which has a fabulous food hall as well as 60 high-end fashion departments.

Knightsbridge, SW1 • Tube: Knightsbridge

Grays Antiques

2 Tucked between Oxford Street and Bond Street, Grays' 200 dealers offer a wide selection of antiques, such as Oriental ceramics, coins, vintage fashion, and teddy bears. A number of dealers, including **The Gilded Lily, Elton Antique Jewellery,** and **Charlotte Sayers,** specialize in jewelry.

58 Davies St. and 1–7 Davies Mews, W1 • tel 020 7629 7034 • Closed Sun.
• Tube: Bond Street • graysantiques.com

Regent Street Shopping

3 Regent Street's facades date from the 19th century, with one major exception—**Liberty's** 1920s black-and-white Tudor-style frontage on the corner of Great Marlborough Street. This much-loved store is synonymous with eclectic fashion and jewelry design, as well as beautiful scarves and fabrics. Regent Street's central section brims with fashion stores, including **Anthropologie** *(No. 158)*, **Hackett** *(Nos. 193–197)*, **Calvin Klein** *(No. 178)*, **Karen Millen** *(No. 247)*, and **Burberry** *(Nos. 121–123)*, plus **Hamleys** *(No. 188–196)* toy store.

Regent St., W1 • Tube: Piccadilly Circus • regentstreetonline.com

Fortnum & Mason

4 For the most civilized way to rest your feet in London, head for the fourth floor of Fortnum & Mason, where the Diamond Jubilee Tea Salon takes afternoon tea very seriously. Sample sumptuous scones served with clotted cream and your choice of preserve, canapés, and a selection of sandwiches. There are also 130 types of tea available. A pianist plays gentle music in the afternoons, while the dress code requests "both sexes lean more towards elegance."

181 Piccadilly, W1 • tel 020 7734 8040 • Closed Jan. 1 and Dec. 25 • ££££
• Tube: Piccadilly Circus • fortnumandmason.com

No. 15 Heritage Bus

5 Jump through the open back of a 1960s-era Routemaster bus, which has been preserved by the city. The No. 15 heritage bus service, whose experienced conductors are happy to answer your questions, runs every 15 minutes on weekends between Trafalgar Square and Tower Hill, along a section of the regular No. 15 route.

Trafalgar Sq. • tel 0343 222 1234 • Closed Oct.–March • Last bus at 6:30 p.m. • £ • tfl.gov.uk

American Bar at The Savoy

6 Abundant olives and snacks are served with expertly mixed cocktails, while a pianist plays classic American jazz in this vibrantly decorated bar, evocative of the 1920s.

Strand • tel 020 7836 4343 • Tube: Charing Cross
• fairmont.com/savoy

Savoy Theatre

7 Finish the day by catching a musical or a lighthearted comedy at this Victorian auditorium, the first to be lit with electricity, which was rebuilt in 1929 in art deco style.

Strand • tel 0844 871 7687 • Tube: Charing Cross • savoytheatre.org

IN **THE KNOW**

Savoy Court, leading to the Savoy Theatre, is the subject of a law forcing traffic to drive on the street's right-hand side, as opposed to the normal left, so theatergoers can exit a taxi and walk straight inside.

WHIRLWIND TOURS

London in a Weekend with Kids

London has a tremendous amount to offer children, from haunted castles to stimulating art and thrilling theme parks.

Chancery Lane

HOLBORN
HOLBORN

HIGH
Holborn

CHARING CROSS RD.
SHAFTESBURY AVE.

ST. GILES

Covent Garden

KINGSWAY

ALDWYCH

FLEET STREET

Temple

STRAND
Leicester Square
STRAND

WATERLOO BRIDGE

Thames

Charing Cross Sta.

Charing Cross
TRAFALGAR SQUARE
Embankment
GOLDEN
JUBILEE BR.

WHITEHALL

London Eye
Waterloo

Waterloo Station

London Dungeon

Westminster
WESTMINSTER BR.
Lambeth North
WESTMINSTER

LAMBETH PALACE RD.

LAMBETH ROAD

KENNINGTON ROAD

LAMBETH BRIDGE
LAMBETH

MILLBANK

ALBERT EMBANKMENT

VAUXHALL

VAUXHALL BRIDGE
Vauxhall
KENNINGTON

Vauxhall Station

❶ London Eye (see pp. 30, 74)
Take a slow whirl on the giant wheel in the sky for a bird's-eye introduction to the United Kingdom's capital. Head south beside the river to the London Dungeon at County Hall.

❷ London Dungeon (see p. 30)
Prepare to be scared at this ghoulish blend of theme park and wax museum. Head back to the London Eye Pier and hop on a river taxi going to Tower Millennium Pier.

**LONDON WITH KIDS, DAY 1   DISTANCE: 5.2 MILES (8.3 KM)
TIME: APPROX. 8 HOURS   TUBE START: WATERLOO**

WHIRLWIND TOURS

3 **Tower of London** (see pp. 30, 168–169) **A thousand years of history come alive inside this riverside castle, once home to kings and queens and now the alleged haunt of many a royal ghost. Head up the stairs by the river to Tower Bridge Approach.**

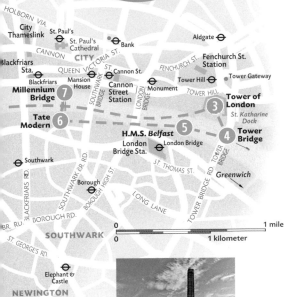

HOLBORN VIA
City
Thameslink   St. Paul's
St. Paul's Cathedral   Bank   Aldgate
Blackfriars Sta.   CANNON   CITY
QUEEN VICTORIA ST.   FENCHURCH ST.   Fenchurch St. Station
Blackfriars   ST. Cannon St.   Tower Hill   Tower Gateway
Millennium Bridge   Mansion House   Cannon Street Station   Monument   TOWER HILL   Tower of London
7   SOUTHWARK BRIDGE   LONDON BRIDGE   **3**   St. Katharine Dock
Tate Modern   **6**   **5**   **4**   Tower Bridge
H.M.S. *Belfast*   London Bridge   TOWER BRIDGE RD
Southwark   London Bridge Sta.   ST. THOMAS ST.   Greenwich
SOUTHWARK ER RD   Borough   LONG LANE
BLACKFRIARS RD   BOROUGH HIGH ST
BR. RU.   BOROUGH RD.
ST. GEORGE'S RD.   SOUTHWARK

0   1 mile
0   1 kilometer

Elephant & Castle
NEWINGTON
LANE   KENNINGTON PARK RD.   Kennington

4 **Tower Bridge** (see pp. 30, 162–163) London's trademark span offers a superb perch from which to photograph the city. After crossing the bridge, turn west along the Queen's Walk.

5 **H.M.S. *Belfast*** (see pp. 30, 171) Battle-tested in several wars, this cruiser shows what life is like on the high seas.

6 **Tate Modern** (see pp. 31, 78–79) Get a crash course in contemporary art inside a massive old power station. Millennium Bridge is just outside.

7 **Millennium Bridge** (see p. 31) Finish the day with a great view of the buildings that line the river, including St. Paul's Cathedral on the north side of the river.

London Eye

① Take the first ride (10 a.m.) and soar 443 feet (135 m) into the morning sky for city views, with the river right at your feet.

Westminster Bridge Rd., SE1 • tel 0870 990 8883 • Closed Dec. 25 • £££££
• Tube: Waterloo • londoneye.com

London Dungeon

② This macabre attraction will scare you to your bones, as actors perform gruesome roles such as Victorian serial killers Jack the Ripper and Sweeney Todd.

Westminster Bridge Rd, SE1 • tel 0333 321 2001 • Closed Dec. 25 • £££££
• Tube: Waterloo • thedungeons.com/london

Tower of London

③ Be dazzled by the Crown Jewels, spooked by tales of ghosts, and regaled with gory stories by the Yeoman Warders.

Tower Hill, EC3 • tel 020 3166 6000 • Closed Jan. 1 and Dec. 25–26 • £££££
• Tube: Tower Hill • hrp.org.uk

WHIRLWIND TOURS

SAVVY **TRAVELER**

The river is the best way to get from the London Eye to the Tower of London. Thames Clippers river taxis *(tel 020 7001 2200, www. thamesclippers.com),* regularly depart from Waterloo Pier next to the Eye.

Tower Bridge

④ Walk over London's most famous bridge, or watch the occasional raising of the roadway that allows large vessels to navigate the Thames.

Tower Bridge Rd., SE1 • tel 020 7403 3761 • Exhibition closed Dec. 24–26 • Exhibition: ££ • Tube: Tower Hill • towerbridge .org.uk

H.M.S. *Belfast*

⑤ Explore this World War II cruiser. Audio guides include a children's version.

Queen's Walk, SE1 • tel 020 7940 6300 • Closed Dec. 24–26 • £££££
• Tube: London Bridge • hmsbelfast.iwm.org.uk

A river cruise from the London Eye to the Tower of London and Tower Bridge.

Tate Modern

6 Older children will love exploring this sprawling gallery of contemporary art. Take them to see Roy Lichtenstein's **"Whaam!"** on Level 5. Its comic-book portrayal of a fighter jet shooting a missile is often appreciated by kids. Younger ones will enjoy the nearby **Under 5s Zone,** which has a musical slide, a cubist-inspired mirrored house, and interactive visual displays.

Bankside, SE1 • tel 020 7887 8888 • Closed Dec. 24–26 • Tube: Southwark • tate.org.uk

Millennium Bridge

7 Cross London's newest bridge (destroyed by Death Eaters in the opening scenes of *Harry Potter and the Half-Blood Prince)* for views of the river and of St. Paul's Cathedral on the north bank. If your kids still have the energy, climb 259 steps to the cathedral's **Whispering Gallery,** where whispers travel around the dome.

Linking Tate Modern and St. Paul's Cathedral, SE1 • Tube: Southwark

DAY **2**

London in a Weekend with Kids

No child visiting London should miss Hamleys toy shop and Pollock's Toy Museum, or the Egyptian mummies at the British Museum.

Euston Sq.

Russell Square

Warren Street

WOBURN PL

BLOOMSBURY

GOWER STREET

SOUTHAMPTON ROW

Great Portland Street

Goodge Street

TOTTENHAM COURT RD

Pollock's Toy Museum ⑦

⑧ **British Museum**

Holborn

Mortimer St.

Tottenham Court Road

NEW OXFORD ST.

HIGH

WIGMORE ST.

REGENT STREET

ST. GILES

SHAFTESBURY AVE.

Covent Garden

London Transport Museum

OXFORD

STREET

Oxford Circus

Hamleys ⑥

SOHO

Covent Garden ④

Bond Street

REGENT STREET

STRAND

MAYFAIR

Piccadilly Circus ⑤

Leicester Square

National Gallery

Charing Cross Embankment

Piccadilly Circus

Trafalgar Square ③

Charing Cross Sta.

ST. JAMES'S

WHITEHALL

PICCADILLY

Green Park

PALL MALL

Horse Guards ②

GREEN PARK

THE MALL

CONSTITUTION HILL

St. James's Park ①

Westminster

WESTMINSTER BR.

BIRDCAGE WALK

St. James's Park ⊖

VICTORIA ST.

BELGRAVIA

Victoria

Victoria Station

HORSEFERRY RD.

WESTMINSTER

LAMBETH BRIDGE

BELGRAVE ROAD

VAUXHALL BRIDGE RD.

MILLBANK

PIMLICO

Pimlico ⊖

VAUXHALL BRIDGE

Vauxhall ⊖

0 [scale] **1 mile**
0 [scale] **1 kilometer**

❶ St. James's Park

(see pp. 34, 138) Snap photos of nearby Buckingham Palace and commune with the resident pelicans in this former royal hunting preserve. Exit the park's east end and cross Horse Guards Road.

❷ Horse Guards

(see pp. 34, 60–61) **Some** of Britain's best pageantry, such as Trooping the Colour and Changing the Guard, are performed on this parade ground. Turn right onto the Mall and duck beneath the imposing Admiralty Arch.

LONDON WITH KIDS, DAY 2   DISTANCE: 3.7 MILES (6 KM)
TIME: APPROX. 8 HOURS   TUBE START: ST JAMES'S PARK

WHIRLWIND TOURS

8 British Museum (see pp. 35, 120–123) **Finish off the day by visiting the ancient statues and Egyptian mummies at one of the world's great museums.**

HOLBORN

Chancery Lane
HOLBORN

HOLBORN VIA

City Thameslink
St. Paul's

FLEET STREET

Temple
Blackfriars Sta.
Blackfriars

VICTORIA EMBANKMENT

Thames

NORTH SOUTHWARK

STAMFORD ST

Waterloo

Waterloo Station

LAMBETH ROAD

LAMBETH

7 Pollock's Toy Museum (see pp. 35, 117) **Travel back to bygone fun and games at a petite museum named after the last of the great Victorian toy-theater makers. Walk south on Tottenham Court Road and east on Great Russell Street.**

6 Hamleys (see p. 35) **Britain's oldest and largest toy store bursts at the seams with amusements for all ages. Continue on Regent Street to Oxford Circus station, and take the Tube two stops to Goodge Street.**

5 Piccadilly Circus (see pp. 35, 90) **Six busy roads come together beneath the giant neon signs and a winged Eros statue hunting for would-be lovers. Follow the broad sweep of Regent Street north from the circus.**

4 Covent Garden (see pp. 34, 102) **This one-time fruit, flower, and vegetable market now blooms with street performers and excellent eateries. Head west on Long Acre to reach Leicester Square and Piccadilly Circus.**

3 Trafalgar Square (see pp. 34, 88) **One has to wonder what Admiral Lord Nelson would say about the rabble-rousers, revelers, and sunbathers who so often inhabit his square. Follow the busy Strand east to Southampton Street, and walk two blocks north.**

St. James's Park

1 This 58-acre (23.4 ha) park is one of London's most kid-friendly spaces. Eat breakfast at **St. James's Café,** where pancakes and a full English breakfast are among the options. There's a playground near the western end, but most children are content to ramble across the lawns, enjoy the views from the Blue Bridge, and see the aquatic birds, especially the pelicans by **Duck Island.**

The Mall, SW1 • tel 0300 061 2350 • Tube: St. James's Park • royalparks.org.uk

IN **THE KNOW**

The first military guard based at Horse Guards was created by King Charles II after the Restoration in 1660 to protect the Palace of Whitehall. The current building dates from 1753 and was the headquarters of the British Army until 1904.

Horse Guards

2 Household Cavalry dressed in smart uniforms parade on a ground where knights once jousted. Changing the Guard takes place daily at 11 a.m. (10 a.m. on Sunday). A museum regales the cavalry's 350-year history.

Whitehall, SW1 • tel 020 7930 3070 • Tube: Westminster or Charing Cross

Trafalgar Square

3 Britain's most renowned public space is a venue for live music, dance performances, art festivals, and annual celebrations. Visit the **National Gallery** (see pp. 92–93), on the north side, to revel in masterpiece art.

Trafalgar Sq., WC2 • Tube: Charing Cross • london.gov.uk/trafalgarsquare

Covent Garden

4 Grab a bite to eat as mimes, acrobats, stunt cyclists, and chainsaw maestros entertain you. If you've got time, visit the **London Transport Museum** (see p. 103) in the market's southeastern corner, where your kids can get behind the wheel of a Tube train simulator and see trains and buses from the 19th century.

Covent Garden Piazza, WC2 • tel 020 7420 5856 • Tube: Covent Garden or Leicester Square • coventgardenlondonuk.com

Piccadilly Circus

5 Famous for its neon signs, the square is also close to kids' favorite **M&M's World**, the world's largest candy store, packed with chocolatey treats and related merchandise (*1 Swiss Court, Leicester Square, WI, tel 020 7025 7171, mymms.com*).

Piccadilly Circus, W1 • Tube: Piccadilly Circus

Hamleys

6 Founded in 1760, this gargantuan toy shop has just about every toy, from the latest doll fashions to Thomas the Tank Engine and London-themed Lego creations. The young staff enjoy showing off the toys, gadgets, and magic tricks, making it lots of fun to walk around the store.

188–196 Regent St., W1 • tel 0371 704 1977 • Closed Easter Sunday & Dec. 25 • Tube: Piccadilly Circus • hamleys.com

Pollock's Toy Museum

7 Vintage toys from around the world fill this small museum. Highlights include Egyptian clay toys, a 19th-century rocking horse, porcelain dolls, dollhouses, and mechanical toys from the olden days.

1 Scala St., W1 • tel 020 7636 3452 • Closed Sun. • ££ • Tube: Goodge Street • pollockstoys.com

British Museum

8 The museum offers several "family trails" as well as hands-on desks, where kids can handle objects from the collection. Young ones will be fascinated by the **Egyptian mummies,** especially the mumified cat (Rooms 62–63), and the **Easter Island heads** (Room 24).

The British Museum provides free activity packs to entertain children during their visit.

38 Russell Sq., WC1 • tel 020 7323 8000 • Closed Jan. 1 and Dec. 24–26 • Tube: Holborn • britishmuseum.org

PART 2

London's Neighborhoods

St. John's Wood

Grand Union Canal

CROWDALE RD.

CAMDEN TOWN

AVENUE ROAD

London Zoo

Mornington Cres.

St. Pancras International (Eurostar)

WELLINGTON RD.

REGENT'S PARK

REGENT'S PARK

British Library

ALBANY

EVERSHOLT ST.

HAMPSTEAD ROAD

Euston Station

GROVE END RD.

ST. JOHN'S WOOD RD.

LISSON GROVE

PARK ROAD

Euston

MAIDA VALE

CLIFTON GDNS.

LITTLE VENICE

Marylebone Station

Madame Tussauds

Regent's Park

EUSTON ROAD

Euston Sq.

WARWICK AVE.

Warwick Ave.

EDGWARE ROAD

Baker St.

Warren Street

Great Portland Street

PARK CRES.

TOTTENHAM COURT RD.

GOWER ST.

Marylebone

BAKER STREET

MARYLEBONE ROAD

PORTLAND PL.

MARYLEBONE

Pollock's Toy Museum

Goodge Street

WESTWAY

GLOUCESTER PL.

Wallace Collection

MORTIMER STREET

BISHOP'S BR. RD.

Paddington Station

Edgware Road

WIGMORE STREET

STREET

Tottenham Court Road

CHARING

Paddington

PRAED STREET

SUSSEX GARDENS

EDGWARE ROAD

Marble Arch

OXFORD

Oxford Circus

SOHO

BAYSWATER

Marble Arch

Speaker's Corner

Trafalgar Square & Soho 84

Bayswater

Lancaster Gate

BAYSWATER ROAD

PARK LANE

MAYFAIR

Royal Academy of Arts

Piccadilly Circus

National Portrait Gallery

Queensway

KENSINGTON

HYDE PARK

PARK LANE

Westminster 54

TRAFALGAR SQUARE

Kensington & South Kensington 126

The Serpentine

Wellington Arch

Green Park

PALL MALL

THE MALL

ST. JAMES'S

St. James's Palace

Kensington Palace

GARDENS

CONSTITUTION HILL

ST. JAMES'S PARK

BIRDCAGE WALK

Royal Albert Hall

EXHIBITION RD.

KNIGHTSBRIDGE

Knightsbridge

GROSVENOR PLACE

Buckingham Palace

Queen's Gallery

St. James's Park

Royal College of Music

Victoria and Albert Museum

BELGRAVE SQUARE

Royal Mews

VICTORIA STREET

WEST

Science Museum

Harrods

SLOANE STREET

BELGRAVIA

Natural History Museum

BROMPTON

BUCKINGHAM PALACE RD.

Victoria

Westminster Cathedral

CROMWELL ROAD

THURLOE PL.

EATON SQ.

BELGRAVE RD.

Victoria Station

Gloucester Road

BROMPTON RD.

South Kensington

Sloane Square

Victoria Coach Station

VAUXHALL BRIDGE RD.

EARLS COURT

Chelsea, Belgravia, & Knightsbridge 142

Pimlico

SOUTH KENSINGTON

FULHAM ROAD

SYDNEY ST.

KING'S ROAD

CHELSEA BR. RD.

PIMLICO

CHELSEA

OAKLEY ST.

ROYAL HOSPITAL RD.

Royal Hospital Chelsea

GROSVENOR ROAD

Thames

Carlyle's House

CHEYNE WALK

ALBERT BRIDGE

BATTERSEA BRIDGE

CHELSEA EMBANKMENT

CHELSEA PHYSIC GARDEN

CHELSEA BRIDGE

QUEENSTOWN ROAD

BATTERSEA PARK RD.

NINE ELM

New Covent Garden Market

BATTERSEA PARK

London's Neighborhoods

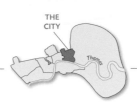

The City

First settled by the Romans around A.D. 50, the oldest part of London is known somewhat confusingly as the City. Covering a little over a square mile (2.6 sq km), with sections of Roman wall still visible, this neighborhood is now a world financial center. Historic buildings, scores of old pubs, and the headquarters of a hundred or so craft guilds, known as livery companies, are located here. Start at the area's highest point, St. Paul's Cathedral, for a view across London from the dome. Admire some of the 47 churches clustered within the square mile, visit Guildhall (the City's ancient seat of government), and explore the Museum of London, the best place to find out about the City's past. On weekdays, the area bustles as almost half a million workers come and go. Evenings and weekends It's quiet- only 10,000 people live here. The buildings may be tightly packed and the main thoroughfares busy, with skyscrapers nudging historic landmarks, but side streets lead to winding medieval lanes, quaint pubs, and leafy churchyards.

❍ **The City's symbol, a griffin holding a shield emblazoned with the Cross of St. George, marks the boundary.**

The City

Nicknamed the Square Mile, the City is easy to get around on foot. Look out for names that describe the trades of old, such as Bread Street and Cloth Fair.

7 Guildhall (see pp. 46–47) For some 800 years, the Guildhall has been the seat of government for the City. Continue along Gresham Street, then turn right onto Aldersgate Street.

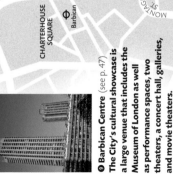

6 Bank of England Museum (see p. 46) Learn all about banking in the capital. Outside, turn left onto Lothbury, which leads onto Gresham Street.

8 Museum of London (see p. 47) **Discover how Londoners have lived from prehistoric times to the 21st century. Outside, turn left onto the Barbican Highwalk.**

9 Barbican Centre (see p. 47) The City's cultural showcase is a large venue that includes the Museum of London as well as performance spaces, two theaters, a concert hall, galleries, and movie theaters.

BISHOPSGATE

FINSBURY CIRCUS

FINSBURY PAVEMENT

MOORGATE STREET

LONDON WALL

CHISWELL STREET

Moorgate Station

Moorgate

Barbican Centre 9

BEECH STREET

ALDERSGATE STREET

Barbican

CHARTERHOUSE SQUARE

Museum of London 8

LONDON WALL

MONTAGUE ST

GRESHAM ST.

Guildhall 7

KING EDWARD ST

NEWGATE ST.

0   400 meters
0   400 yards

❶ St. Paul's Cathedral (see pp. 48–49) Climb to the dome of this monumental church, designed by Sir Christopher Wren, for a fabulous view of London. Behind St. Paul's, cross New Change (past a new shopping mall) onto Watling Street, then turn left onto Queen Victoria Street.

❷ Mansion House (see p. 44) Admire the official home of the Lord Mayor of London, then turn right and walk down King William Street and turn left onto Monument Street.

❸ Monument (see p. 44) Climb to the top of this monument to the Great Fire of 1666. Afterward continue on Monument Street, turn left onto Botolph Street to Lime Street, and take Lime Passage to Leadenhall Market.

❹ Lloyd's Building (see p. 45) Crane your neck to view this strikingly modern glass building. Walk around Lloyd's, turn left onto Leadenhall Street, and follow Cornhill to Threadneedle Street.

❼ Leadenhall Market (see p. 45) Stroll under the cast-iron roof of this colorful Victorian market hall, browsing its upscale shops and restaurants. From the market, take Leadenhall Place back to Lime Street and turn left.

THE CITY DISTANCE: 5.3 MILES (8.5 KM) TIME: APPROX. 5–7 HOURS
TUBE START: ST. PAUL'S OR MANSION HOUSE

St. Paul's Cathedral

1 See pp. 48–49.

St. Paul's Churchyard, EC4 • tel 020 7236 4128 • Sunday: Open for worship only • £££££ • Tube: St. Paul's or Mansion House • www.stpauls.co.uk

GOOD **EATS**

■ **THE ANTHOLOGIST**
Just steps away from the Bank of England, this chic and airy bistro boasts a quintessentially English deli, plus tasty treats from club sandwiches to prawn lollipops, as well as a kid's menu. **58 Gresham St., EC2, tel 0845 468 0101, £**

■ **SKY POD BAR**
At the top of the "Walkie-Talkie," this café in the Sky Garden has far-reaching views and serves paninis, salads, soups, coffee, and cakes. **20 Fenchurch Street, EC3, tel 0333 772 0020, £**

■ **SWEETINGS**
Crab soup, oysters, and smoked eel are usually on the menu in this restaurant, which has changed little in more than a hundred years. **39 Queen Victoria St., EC4, tel 020 7248 3062, ££**

Mansion House

2 The Lord Mayor of London lives in this Georgian palace. Elected for a one-year term by the City of London Corporation, the Lord Mayor acts as the City's unpaid ambassador. Built to flaunt the City's wealth and power, the **Salon** sparkles with chandeliers, while the former ballroom and 90-foot-long (27 m) **Great Egyptian Room** hosts social functions. Treasures include 17th-century Dutch paintings, gold and silver-plate candelabra, bowls, and flagons, and the Lord Mayor's sword and mace.

Mansion House Place, EC4 • tel 020 7626 2500 • Closed Aug. and bank holidays • ££ (tours only: Tues. p.m.; Walbrook entrance) • Tube: Bank or Cannon Street • cityoflondon.gov.uk

Monument

3 Crowned with a golden flame, this Roman Doric column designed by Sir Christopher Wren celebrates the regeneration of the City after the Great Fire of 1666. The fire, which began in a bakery on Pudding Lane, raged for four days and destroyed most of the City's buildings. Laid on its side, the 202-foot (61 m) structure would reach the spot where the bakery stood. A climb up 311 steps leads to a **viewing gallery**. Those unable to make the climb can see a **webcam panorama** in the lobby.

Monument St., EC3 • tel 020 7626 2717 • Closed: Jan. 1 and Dec. 24–26 • £ • Tube: Monument • themonument.info

Leadenhall Market

4 Built at the eastern end of the Roman Basilica, Leadenhall is not only one of London's oldest markets but also the most colorful. Popular at lunchtime with City workers, the beautiful Victorian building has several bars and restaurants, such as the **Lamb Tavern**, dating from 1780. Quality retail outlets include tailors **Reiss** *(no. 26)*, **The Pen Shop** *(nos. 8–9)* for fine writing implements, and **Amathus** *(nos. 17–19)*, selling rare wines and liqueurs. Fresh food is still sold and the hooks on which game and poultry were once hung high on the walls help retain the market's cornucopian air.

Gracechurch St., EC3 • Tube: Monument, Bank
• leadenhallmarket.co.uk

Stroll through the vaulted halls of Leadenhall Market, a hub for upscale food and wine stores, bars, and restaurants.

Lloyd's Building

5 This 1984 building includes an 84-foot-high (26 m) central atrium. Designed by Richard Rogers, co-architect of the groundbreaking Pompidou Centre in Paris, it is the home of Lloyd's of London, the world's leading market for insurers, which began as an informal business in Lloyd's coffee shop in 1688. Two remnants of Lloyd's history are the **Adam Room**, designed by the architect Robert Adam in 1763 as a dining room for the Earl of Shelburne, on the 11th floor, and the **Lutine bell**, the centerpiece of the atrium. Salvaged from the British warship H.M.S. *Lutine* in 1799, it was rung to announce news on ships insured by members of Lloyd's. Today it is not used except in times of national mourning, such as the death of a member of the royal family.

1 Lime St., EC3 • tel 020 7327 1000 • £££ (tours for business-related groups only; advance reservation required) • Tube: Monument or Bank • lloyds.com

Bank of England Museum

6 Look up from what appears to be an impenetrable stone bastion at street level to see the great mansion housing the Bank of England above. Its museum, peopled by costumed wax figures, features items stretching back 300 years. These include real and forged banknotes, gold bars, documents, and weights.

Bartholomew Lane, EC2 • tel 020 7601 5545 • Closed Sat.–Sun. & bank holidays • Tube: Bank • bankofengland.co.uk/museum

Guildhall

7 For more than 800 years, elected merchants and financiers have held court and laid down the law here. The huge medieval **Great Hall,** built in 1411 and rebuilt after bomb damage in 1941, is still used as a banquet hall. Its windows show the names of London mayors since 1189. Wooden statues of the giants Gog and

The annual Pearly Kings and Queens Harvest Festival celebrations begin at Guildhall.

THE CITY

Magog, mythical founders of the City, are paraded in the annual Lord Mayor's Show (see p. 52). The circle of colored stones in the courtyard in front of the Guildhall marks the site of the old **Roman Amphitheater.** Its scant remains can be seen in the basement of the adjacent **Guildhall Art Gallery,** which displays paintings of London going back 400 years and thematic pictures of Victorian life.

Gresham St., EC2 • tel 020 7332 1313, Art Gallery: 020 7332 3700 • call for opening hours, as there are many functions here; Art Gallery: closed Sun. a.m. • Tube: Bank or St. Paul's • www.guildhall.cityoflondon.gov.uk

Museum of London

8 This is the place to learn about the history of the capital, from its origins as a settlement on the banks of the Thames to the present. Highlights include a gallery devoted to the **Great Fire** of 1666 and the red and gold **Lord Mayor's Coach,** still used once a year but built more than 250 years ago. Costumes, oral histories, shop interiors, and scenes such as the **Victorian Walk** depict the lives of Londoners through the ages.

150 London Wall, EC2 • tel 020 7001 9844 • Closed Dec. 24–26 • Tube: Barbican, St. Paul's, or Moorgate • museumoflondon.org.uk

SAVVY **TRAVELER**

Unlock a Sherlockian mystery as you explore London with the Museum of London's "A Hollow Body" interactive app. Designed to be used by pairs, its evocative narration profiles the city streets.

Barbican Centre

9 Constructed in the 1970s on a site bombed in World War II, the Barbican Centre is part of a larger residential complex named for a long lost city fortification. The **Lakeside Terrace** provides a tranquil place to relax in the heart of the City. Inside the building, two theaters, a concert hall (home of the **London Symphony Orchestra**), two art galleries, and three movie theaters hum with activity.

Silk St., EC2 • tel 020 7638 4141; box office: 020 7638 8891 • £££–£££££ • Tube: Barbican or Moorgate • barbican.org.uk

St. Paul's Cathedral

The crowning glory of the City, this domed cathedral church took
35 years to complete and is an architectural masterpiece.

Pale Portland stone was transported by boat from Dorset for the construction of St. Paul's.

London's Anglican cathedral, the first to be built for the English Protestant faith, is a marvel of architectural engineering and a fitting monument to the genius of its architect, Sir Christopher Wren. After the Great Fire of London destroyed its more conventional predecessor in 1666, Wren was left to devise an entirely new building in the style of his own time—English baroque. The result, completed in 1710, is a majestic space of marble and mosaics, soaring to a triumphant dome.

■ CELEBRATIONS & MEMORIALS

From the top of Ludgate Hill, the front of St. Paul's Cathedral is an imposing sight, its steps leading up to the 30-foot-high (9 m) **Great West Door.** Used for ceremonial occasions, such as the 1981 wedding of Lady Diana Spencer to Prince Charles, St. Paul's contains monuments to national heroes, including the **Duke of Wellington** (in the nave) and **Admiral Lord Nelson** (in the South Transept).

■ EXQUISITE EMBELLISHMENTS

The church is built in the shape of a cross. Ceiling mosaics were added after Queen Victoria described the building as "dreary, dingy and undevotional." The **choir stalls** were decorated by Britain's best-known wood carver, the 18th-century master Grinling Gibbons, and the magnificent gilded **wrought-iron work** throughout the cathedral is by a French master metalworker, Jean Tijou. The **high altar** was made in 1958, with a canopy based on a sketch by Wren. Also in 1958, the **American Memorial Chapel** behind the altar was opened, with a roll of honor to the 28,000 Americans who died in the defense of Europe during World War II.

■ THE DOME

At 365 feet (111 m) high, the dome is almost as tall as St. Peter's Basilica in Vatican City. The first stop after climbing 257 spiraling steps is the **Whispering Gallery,** so called because if you whisper something while facing the wall, someone on the opposite side of the gallery, 105 feet (32 m) away, can hear you clearly. From here you can see the paintings of St. Paul by James Thornhill that decorate the dome. Climb another 271 steps to the external **Golden Gallery** for views across London.

■ THE CRYPT

The **Duke of Wellington** and **Admiral Lord Nelson,** Napoleon's vanquishers, are both entombed in the crypt. Many well-known names are honored here, including Wren himself. His epitaph ends: "Reader, if you seek his monument, look around you."

SAVVY **TRAVELER**

The crypt contains a good café serving hot and cold food, a restaurant, and an area to sit and relax. The entrance is on the north side of the church, and you don't need a ticket to visit.

St. Paul's Churchyard, EC4 • tel 020 7236 4128 • Closed Sun. except for worship (free) • £££££ • Tube: St. Paul's or Mansion House • stpauls.co.uk

THE CITY

THE CITY

Wren Churches

Within the square mile that defines the City of London an exceptional group of churches charts the evolving story of ecclesiastical architecture in England. Some survive from medieval times, but most are linked with Sir Christopher Wren, the scientist turned architect responsible for rebuilding 51 of the 80 churches destroyed in the Great Fire of 1666. Many were restored after World War I damage, and they provide ideal venues for lunchtime concerts.

Sir Christopher Wren appears in a stained-glass window in St. Lawrence Jewry (above); beside St. Mary-le-Bow (right) is a statue of parishioner John Smith (1580–1631), founder of Jamestown, Virginia.

Inventive Designs

Rising from the ashes of the Great Fire, Sir Christopher Wren's churches represented an innovative style that suited the new Protestant way of worship of the time. Central to his design was an interior where, in his words, the congregation could "hear distinctly and see the preacher."

Classical Look

Construction of **St. Mary-le-Bow** (*Cheapside, EC2, tel 020 7248 5139, closed Sat.–Sun., stmarylebow .co.uk*), one of the first churches to be rebuilt, began just two years after the fire. Wren's classical 224-foot-high (68 m) steeple set the standard for other architects. (Londoners have a special affection for this church since only those born within the sound of Bow bells are said to be true Cockneys.)

One of the most splendid of the Wren churches is **St. Mary Abchurch** (*Abchurch La., EC4, tel 020 7626 0306, closed Thurs.–Sat., london-city-churches .org.uk*). Completed in 1686, it reveals Wren's genius for turning a small space into a thing of splendor.

The dome over the nave is invisible from the outside, giving an effect described by the poet John Betjeman as "both uplifting and intimate." Among its other glories is a reredos by Grinling Gibbons, the sculptor and wood-carver who worked on St. Paul's Cathedral (see pp. 48–49).

Prototype Dome

St. Stephen Walbrook *(Walbrook, EC4, tel 020 7626 9000, closed Sat.–Sun., ststephenwalbrook.net)* was the first domed church in Britain. It would have had special meaning for Wren as his own parish church—he lived at No. 15 Walbrook at the time. The ornate dome, supported by eight Corinthian pillars and arches, acted as a prototype for St. Paul's.

The Guild Church of the Corporation of London, **St. Lawrence Jewry** *(Guildhall Yd., EC2, tel 020 7600 9478, closed Sat.–Sun., stlawrencejewry.org .uk)*, on Gresham Street, stands near Guildhall (see pp. 46–47). See the stained-glass windows in the vestibule depicting Wren, Gibbons, and master mason Edward Strong, the men who created these churches.

Celebrations

Throughout the year, musicians, dancers, and performance artists take to the streets and parks, and competing crews head out onto the River Thames itself for an annual round of festivals and events. Some events celebrate modern London's diverse ethnic mix; others are decades or even centuries old.

■ LORD MAYOR'S SHOW
The Lord Mayor's Show harkens back 800 years to the days of King John, when the newly elected Lord Mayor traveled by river barge from the City to Westminster to pledge his allegiance to the Crown. On a Saturday each November, marching bands, floats, musicians, and dancers now start at Guildhall, then pass St. Paul's on their way to the Royal Courts of Justice, where the Lord Mayor takes the oath of allegiance. The day ends with fireworks over the Thames at 5 p.m.

Nov. • Tube: Bank, St. Paul's, or Temple • lordmayorsshow.org

■ TOTALLY THAMES
This month-long festival in September celebrates the best arts and music the capital has to offer. Nearly 200 river-related events include stage performances, art installations, bands, and dancing, with food stalls taking

over the riverbank from Westminster to Tower Bridge. The festival culminates in a night carnival and fireworks display.

Sept. • Tube: Waterloo, Embankment, London Bridge, or Tower Hill • totallythames.org

■ NEW YEAR'S DAY PARADE & FESTIVAL
Marching bands, dancers, and street performers parade through Piccadilly Circus, Trafalgar Square, and Whitehall to Parliament Street on New Year's Day.

12 Noon Jan. 1 • Tube: Piccadilly Circus or Charing Cross • lnydp.com

■ CHINESE NEW YEAR
Celebrations are held on the weekend after Chinese New Year (a lunar festival, Chinese New Year falls on a different date each year). Enjoy colorful lion dances, acrobats, parading dragons, and food stalls in and around Gerrard Street, or head for Trafalgar Square to

Traditionally, Watermen took the Lord Mayor by barge to take his oath; today they go on foot.

listen to Chinese music and dance on a giant stage.

Jan. or Feb. • Tube: Leicester Square
• visitlondon.com

■ THE NOTTING HILL CARNIVAL
Europe's largest street event celebrates the dynamic and diverse Afro-Caribbean community in London. Held on the last weekend in August, the three-day street party begins on Saturday, when steel bands compete for the title "Champions of Steel." Sunday is the Kids' Carnival and Monday the carnival parade. Expect huge crowds, flamboyant costumes,

lavish floats, loud reggae and calypso music, and thousands of performers.

Aug. • Tube: Notting Hill Gate or Ladbroke Grove • nhcarnival.org

■ THE BOAT RACE
Begun in 1829, this annual race is part of the rivalry between the universities of Oxford and Cambridge. Eight-man boats row the 4-mile (6.4 km) course in west London from Putney Bridge to Chiswick Bridge. Join the cheering spectators on the riverbank, or watch the race from a waterside pub.

March or April • Tube: Hammersmith or Putney Bridge • theboatrace.org

WESTMINSTER

Westminster

All the pomp and ceremony of London is centered around Westminster, perched on the north bank of the Thames and bounded by Hyde Park to the west and Regent Street to the east. Stand in Parliament Square to see the twin pillars of the British establishment: Westminster Abbey, where kings and queens are crowned, and the Palace of Westminster, better known as the Houses of Parliament, where elected governments come and go. Through the trees in nearby St. James's Park you can see Buckingham Palace. On special occasions, members of the royal family appear on the palace balcony. Heading north from Parliament Square, the wide avenue of Whitehall passes near the subterranean Churchill War Rooms. On the west side of Whitehall, Horse Guards Parade provides a grand setting for royal ceremonies such as Trooping the Colour. Away from the politics and pageantry, great art collections vie for attention with some of London's smartest shops and swankiest restaurants in the elegant surroundings of Piccadilly and Mayfair.

❍ **Westminster Abbey's massive, soaring West Towers, added in the 18th century, were designed by architect Nicholas Hawksmoor.**

WESTMINSTER

8 Wallace Collection (see pp. 62–63) Enjoy the fine collection of European paintings, furniture, and decorative art. Retrace your steps to Oxford Street, and walk west through throngs of shoppers toward Hyde Park.

9 Marble Arch (see p. 63) The former gateway to Buckingham Palace now stands in splendid isolation at the west end of Oxford Street. Head south down Park Lane, then left onto Curzon Street and Shepherd Market.

7 Handel & Hendrix in London (see p. 62) See exhibits relating to the lives of George Frideric Handel and Jimi Hendrix. Continue on Brook Street, then turn right onto Duke Street.

10 Shepherd Market (see p. 63) An eclectic mix of pubs, restaurants, and boutiques fills the narrow streets of this lively part of Mayfair.

1 Buckingham Palace (see p. 58) Start at the Queen's London home for the daily ceremony of Changing the Guard. Explore the Queen's Gallery and Royal Mews. Then go along the south side of St. James's Park on Birdcage Walk to Parliament Square.

WESTMINSTER

WESTMINSTER   DISTANCE: 4 MILES (6.4 KM)   TIME: APPROX. 8 HOURS
TUBE START: HYDE PARK CORNER, GREEN PARK, OR VICTORIA

Westminster

Some of the nation's best known buildings cluster in this one corner of London.

6 Royal Academy of Arts (see p. 61) View the small permanent collection or see a blockbuster visiting exhibit before heading north again along Old Bond Street and left onto Brook Street to the Handel & Hendrix in London.

5 Horse Guards (see pp. 60–61) Leave the headquarters of the Household Cavalry, and with St. James's Park on your left, head north to Piccadilly to the Royal Academy of Arts.

4 Churchill War Rooms (see p. 60) Visit Churchill's World War II bunker, then go up Whitehall to Horse Guards Parade.

3 Houses of Parliament (see pp. 58–59) Once you have seen the "mother of parliaments", stop to admire the view from Westminster Bridge, then cross Parliament Square to Great George Street

2 Westminster Abbey (see pp. 64–65) See where monarchs have been crowned and buried for nearly a thousand years, then go along the side of Parliament Square and cross St. Margaret Street to the Houses of Parliament.

Buckingham Palace

1 Old Master paintings, furniture, and porcelain from the Royal Collection decorate Buckingham Palace's 19 **State Rooms,** which open to the public each mid-July–September. A visit to this 775-room mansion is otherwise rewarded by the sight of changing guards (see p. 67) or even a glimpse of a member of the royal family swooping past in the back of a limousine. See the new guard marching to the palace from Wellington Barracks, to the left of the palace as you face it, each morning. **St. James's Park** is a good viewing point. On the south side of the Palace, the **Queen's Gallery** houses changing exhibitions of works from the Royal Collection, which was acquired by the present Queen's predecessors more than 400 years ago and is held in trust by her for the nation. Just beyond the gallery are the **Royal Mews,** home to the Windsor Grey horses that draw the Queen's carriage. The Gold State Coach used for coronations and other grand state occasions, seven other historic carriages used for ceremonial occasions, and the gold-braided state livery worn by coachmen and equerries show how the royals travel.

The Mall, SW1 • tel 020 7766 7300 • State Rooms: open mid-July–Sept. (dates change yearly), exclusive tours (£££££) can be booked outside the summer opening season, £££££ • Queen's Gallery: Closed public holidays, £££ • Royal Mews: Open Feb.–Nov., £££ • Tube: Hyde Park Corner, Green Park, or Victoria • royalcollection. org.uk

Westminster Abbey

2 See pp. 64–65.

Broad Sanctuary, SW1 • tel 020 7222 5152 • Sun.: Open for worship only, free • £££££ • Tube: Westminster • westminster-abbey.org

Houses of Parliament

3 Opposite Westminster Abbey stands the familiar Victorian, neo-Gothic Palace of Westminster, built after fire destroyed its predecessor in 1834. Listen for **Big Ben,** the great bell that strikes every hour, with four smaller bells striking the quarters, from the

Statues of kings and queens fill the Central Lobby of the Houses of Parliament.

Elizabeth Tower at the building's northern end (both are closed for restoration into 2021). At its southern end is the **Victoria Tower,** which was the tallest secular structure in the world when it was completed in 1858. The Queen uses the Sovereign's Entrance at the base of the tower for the annual State Opening of Parliament in spring.

The entrance for visitors, and for tours, is on Cromwell Green, which leads to the **Great Hall,** the historic heart of the building. Dating from 1097, this has the largest timber roof in northern Europe, and beneath its ancient beams countless laws have been passed, trials held, and coronation breakfasts eaten. When parliament is in session, visitors can attend debates and watch committees. The **House of Lords,** the upper chamber, is to the right of the lobby inside the St. Stephen's entrance. To the left is the **House of Commons,** the chamber where elected Members of Parliament (MPs) sit.

Parliament Square, SW1 • tel 020 7219 4114 • Tube: Westminster • parliament.uk

Churchill War Rooms

4 During World War II, Sir Winston Churchill and his cabinet directed military operations from an underground bunker between Parliament Square and the Prime Minister's residence at 10 Downing Street. Churchill had his own room with a desk and bed, although he slept there on only three occasions. He delivered some of

his major wartime speeches from the desk in 1940, as London came under ferocious bombardment. Beside the bed is an ashtray, creating a lingering feeling that Churchill, smoking one of his famous cigars, has just left the room. The other rooms are preserved much as they were at the height of the conflict. In the **Cabinet Room,** the chiefs of staff made decisions, and in the **Map Room,** Army, Navy, and Air Force officers notched up the scores of planes shot down in the Battle of Britain and followed the ebb and flow of numerous other battles. Churchill kept in touch with the White House from the **transatlantic telephone room,** converted from a broom closet.

The Map Room—its walls covered with maps, charts, and notes—was the hub of Churchill's World War II bunker.

King Charles St., SW1 • tel 020 7930 6961 • Closed Dec. 24–26 • £££££ • Tube: Westminster or St. James's Park • wm.org.uk/visits/churchill-war-rooms

Horse Guards

5 Farther up Whitehall toward Trafalgar Square, past Downing Street, this ensemble of buildings replaced the former Palace of Whitehall, which burned down in the 1690s. Today Horse Guards is famous for the mounted soldiers from the Household Cavalry who stand guard in plumed hats and thigh-high boots, swords drawn. The old jousting yard is now **Horse Guards Parade,** an open space used for ceremonies such as the Queen's birthday parade in June, better known as **Trooping the Colour** (see p. 67).

The Household Cavalry mounts the guard at Horse Guards between 10 a.m and 4 p.m., and the guard changes at 11 a.m (10 a.m. on Sunday). A Dismounting Ceremony takes place at 4 p.m. You can also see the troopers tending their horses in the 18th-century stables that are part of the **Household Cavalry Museum.** Here, you can find out about the two Household Cavalry regiments, which have provided an escort for the monarch for 350 years and also continue to serve queen and country in conflicts around the world.

Whitehall, SW1 • tel 020 7930 3070 • Closed Dec. 24–26 • £££ • Tube: Westminster or Piccadilly Circus • householdcavalrymuseum.co.uk

Royal Academy of Arts

6 Privately funded and independently run, the Royal Academy on Piccadilly is Britain's premier artists' society. It occupies **Burlington House,** the last remaining 17th-century noble mansion on Piccadilly, on the far side of a large fountain-filled courtyard. Free tours of the historic building, including the **John Madejski Fine Rooms,** provide a background to the workings of the Academy, with pictures from its collection on view. Major international loan exhibitions are put on throughout the year, but the highlight is the **Summer Exhibition,** an annual show of paintings, prints, and sculpture by Academicians and members of the public. Anyone can submit work for consideration by the hanging committee, and successful applicants have the thrill of seeing their creations on show near that of Academicians such as David Hockney and Tracey Emin.

Piccadilly, W1 • tel 020 7300 8000 • Loan exhibitions: £££ • Tube: Piccadilly Circus or Green Park • royalacademy.org.uk

---

GOOD **EATS**

■ **ST. JAMES CAFÉ**
A delightful setting by the lake in St James's Park makes this a good stopping-off point for snacks, coffee and ice cream.
St. James's Park, SW1, tel 020 7839 1149, ££

■ **NOPI**
Yotam Ottolenghi is one of the hottest chefs in town, and his flagship restaurant serves Mediterranean food and sharing plates, including interesting vegetarian options.
21–22 Warwick St., W1, tel 020 7494 9584, ££££

■ **THE WOLSELEY**
Both opulent and elegant, this former marble-floored car showroom built in the 1920s serves delicious lunches.
160 Piccadilly, W1, tel 020 7499 6996, ££

WESTMINSTER

WESTMINSTER

Handel & Hendrix in London

7 At the southern end of South Moulton Street is the lovingly restored Georgian house where George Frideric Handel lived and worked from 1723 until his death in 1759. Handel wrote some of his best-loved compositions here, including the *Messiah* and the *Music for the Royal Fireworks*. American rock legend Jimi Hendrix lived next door (1968–69) in a flat furnished exactly as it was back then, with period knickknacks from the Portobello Road market.

25 Brook St., W1 • tel 020 7495 1685 • ££ • Closed Sun. and some public holidays • Tube: Bond Street • handelhouse.org

The Wallace Collection

8 This elegant building and art collection on Manchester Square seem far removed from the busy shops of nearby Oxford Street. The first Marquess of Hertford began the collection in the 18th century

The Wallace Collection holds more than 500 pieces of French porcelain and furniture.

with portraits of his children by Sir Joshua Reynolds and six paintings by the Venetian painter, Canaletto. Paintings from such masters as Rembrandt, Titian, and Velázquez grace the walls. Fragonard's "The Swing" and Poussin's "Dance to the Music of Time" stand out among the many French paintings. Other treasures include furniture by the 18th-century French cabinetmaker André-Charles Boulle and the finest collection of arms and armor in the United Kingdom.

Manchester Square, W1 • tel 020 7563 9500 • Closed Dec. 24–26 • Tube: Bond Street or Marble Arch • wallacecollection.org

Marble Arch

9 Isolated on a traffic island where Oxford Street and Park Lane meet, this triumphal arch was originally built as an entrance to Buckingham Palace and moved here in 1851. Made of Carrera marble and based on the ancient Roman triumphal arch of the emperor Constantine, the arch serves no useful purpose, although it was once used as a police station: From here, officers could keep an eye on **Speaker's Corner** in nearby Hyde Park, a place where anyone can stand up and say what they like. Marble Arch also marks the location of the old Tyburn Tree, site of public hangings until 1783.

Intersection of Oxford St. and Park Lane • Tube: Marble Arch

IN **THE KNOW**

The route from Newgate Prison to the Tyburn gallows followed the course that Oxford Street does now and was known as Tyburn Way. Stalls were set up to serve the crowds who came to watch the hangings.

WESTMINSTER

Shepherd Market

10 Just off Curzon Street, village-like Shepherd Market is an ancient corner of Mayfair (toward its western side) whose small streets are lined with 18th-century houses. This area was the site of the May Fair, an annual fortnight of revelry, banned in 1708, that gave the area its name. Shepherd Market has small, mostly high-end shops and restaurants and several Victorian pubs.

Between Curzon St. and Piccadilly • Tube: Green Park • shepherdmarket.co.uk

Westminster Abbey

*This glorious building sums up all the
pageantry of English history.*

The Choir of Westminster Abbey performs in front of the 19th-century choir screen in the nave.

London's most beautiful building is also its oldest, dating back to a monastery founded in A.D. 960 by 12 Benedictine monks on the banks of the Thames. In the 11th century, King Edward the Confessor built a new, larger abbey and monastery. This, in turn, was replaced by the present Gothic building, started by King Henry III in 1245. Some buildings from Edward's monastery still survive, including parts of nearby Westminster School. The abbey Choir School's 30 boys take part in the daily choral services.

■ High Altar

From the north entrance, walk ahead and look to the left to see the high altar above a colorful mosaic pavement from 1268. Behind the altar, **St. Edward's Chapel** commemorates King Edward the Confessor, whose newly built abbey was consecrated in 1065, a year before his death, and who was canonized in 1161. The chapel contains Edward's shrine and the tombs of several other monarchs.

■ Henry VII's Lady Chapel

Visit the jewel-like Henry VII's Lady Chapel: Its fan vaulting has the delicacy of lace. Henry belonged to the House of Tudor, whose emblem graces the bronze gates. The king's tomb, with that of his wife, Elizabeth of York, lies behind the altar. In the **north aisle** of the chapel are the colorful tombs of Queen Elizabeth I and her half-sister, Queen Mary. Sworn enemies divided by religion in life, they are united in death. In the **south aisle** lies the tomb of King George II, the last king to be buried in the abbey (in 1760).

■ Poets' Corner

In the **South Transept,** this area celebrates the lives of poets and playwrights, as well as other contributors

SAVVY **TRAVELER**

For a view over the abbey, visit the roof terrace of **Central Hall Westminster** (*Storey's Gate, SW1, 020 7222 8010, c-h-w.com*), a conference center and Methodist church on Parliament Square.

to British culture. Shakespeare and Lord Byron have monuments, while Dr. Samuel Johnson and Charles Dickens are buried here, as is composer George Frideric Handel. The ashes of actor Sir Laurence Olivier are also interred here.

■ Nave

One hundred and fifty years in the building, the 102-foot-high (31 m) nave is the tallest in England. Among those buried here are Charles Darwin, author of *On the Origin of Species,* and the scientist, Sir Isaac Newton. Beneath the west window is the tomb of the **Unknown Warrior,** representing all those who died fighting in World War I. In St. George's Chapel, on the south side, the high-backed, solid oak **Coronation Chair** rests on four gilt lions. Since 1308, all but two monarchs (King Edward V and King Edward VIII) have been crowned in it.

WESTMINSTER

Broad Sanctuary, SW1 • tel 020 7222 5152 • Sunday: Open for worship only, free • £££££ • Tube: Westminster • westminster-abbey.org

Royal City

Since the days of the Anglo-Saxon king Edward the Confessor, monarchs have added grandeur and glamour to London, choosing it for their power base, shaping its appearance with lavish palaces, and providing scenes of spectacle and pageantry. Royal palaces are rich in history and tradition, and several provide the setting for colorful and spectacular ceremonies whose origins lie deep in the past.

Prince William and Kate Middleton (above) wed in April 2011 in Westminster Abbey; the Tower of London's White Tower (right) was completed in 1097.

Center of Government

When William the Conqueror invaded England in 1066, Winchester in Hampshire was the country's capital. London, however, was the largest city, and William knew he must control it. He chose Edward the Confessor's newly finished **Westminster Abbey** (see pp. 64–65) for his coronation and built the White Tower, the central feature of the **Tower of London** (see pp. 168–169).

In the 12th century, the first Palace of Westminster, to which King William II had added the **Great Hall** (see p. 59), became the main royal residence in London.

Succession of Palaces

In the 16th century, King Henry VIII made the Palace of Whitehall his principal residence. Previously known as York House, it had belonged to Cardinal Wolsey. Henry renamed and extended Whitehall and added a jousting yard—now the site of Horse Guards Parade. In 1622, King James I added **Banqueting House** (*Whitehall SW1*,

WESTMINSTER

tel 020 3166 6154/5, closed Sun., public holidays, and Dec. 24–Jan. 1, ££, hrp.org.uk), built to a design by Inigo Jones, who also built the **Queen's House** at Greenwich. Banqueting House has a ceiling painting by Peter Paul Rubens, commissioned by King Charles I, which survived intact when a fire destroyed the rest of Whitehall Palace in 1698.

Less than a mile (1 km) from Banqueting House, the northern gatehouse of **St. James's Palace** *(royal.gov.uk)* is one of central London's few Tudor landmarks. King Henry VIII constructed the palace in the 1530s and used it mainly for receiving royal envoys. Even now, ambassadors to the United Kingdom are accredited to the Court of St. James.

In 1761, King George III bought Buckingham House, and in 1828 King George IV asked architect John Nash to transform it into a palace. When Victoria became queen in 1837, the work was unfinished. She moved in nevertheless, and **Buckingham Palace** (see p. 58) has been the official London royal residence ever since.

ROYAL **CEREMONIES**

Changing the Guard
Each morning, the guard at Buckingham Palace is replaced. **Buckingham Palace (see p. 58), daily 11 a.m.–noon, changing-the-guard.com**

Trooping the Colour The Foot Guards celebrate the Queen's official birthday by trooping their regimental flag through the ranks. **Horse Guards Parade (see pp. 60–61), a Sat. in June, householddivision.org.uk**

Ceremony of the Keys The Tower of London's gates are locked for the night. **Tower of London (see pp. 168–169), nightly, hrp.org.uk**

Beating Retreat A member of the royal family takes the salute. **Horse Guards Parade (see pp. 60–61), two evenings in June, householddivision.org.uk**

WESTMINSTER

Mayfair's Posh Shops

Mayfair, in the northern reaches of Westminster, offers the choicest in upmarket specialty stores, many of which have been operating for hundreds of years. Whether your fancy is window-shopping or splurging on treats, here you will find the perfect jewel, artwork, or handmade truffle.

■ BOND STREET

A mere half-mile (1 km) long, Bond Street offers a heady shopping experience. In addition to the flagship outlets of major fashion brands, including relative newcomer **Dior** *(No. 160)*, you'll find jewelers and antique dealers. Diamonds sparkle in the windows of **De Beers** *(No. 45–50)*, and **Asprey** *(No. 167)* sells luggage as well as jewelry. View an auction at **Bonhams** *(No. 101)* or **Sotheby's** *(Nos. 34–35)*, or drop into a high-end gallery such as **Richard Green** *(No. 147)* or the **Halcyon Gallery** *(Nos. 144–146)*.

Tube: Bond Street or Green Park
• bondstreetassociation.co.uk

■ CORK STREET

More art awaits in Cork Street's elegant galleries east of Bond Street. **Redfern** *(No. 20)* represents more than 20 contemporary artists and their estates, among them Patrick Procktor and the sculptor Lisa Lombardi. Stop at **Flowers** *(No. 21)*, where you might spot a John Kirby print or Jiro Osuga painting, while **Messum's** *(No. 28)* specializes in British artists such as Graham Sutherland and members of the St. Ives School. An ongoing redevelopment project has invigorated Cork Street with innovative new galleries, such as **Nahmad Projects** *(No. 2)* performing art space.

Tube: Piccadilly • corkstgalleries.com

■ BURLINGTON ARCADE

Just south of Cork Street, this glass-roofed shopping avenue twinkles with antique silver, jewelry, and high-end watches. Opened in 1819, it was Britain's first shopping arcade and remains a treasure trove of specialist stores. Pop into **N. Peal** *(Nos. 37–40)* for cashmere sweaters. Try the private profiling room for perfume at **Penhaligon's** *(Nos. 16–17)* and **Maison Michel** *(No. 46)*

WESTMINSTER

Shop for luxury treats in elegant surroundings at Burlington Arcade.

for ready-to-wear and bespoke hats. Guards in top hats patrol the arcade on the lookout for unruly behavior such as whistling and running.

Tube: Piccadilly • burlington-arcade.co.uk

■ Savile Row
The world's premier street for custom-made gentlemen's tailoring is lined with Georgian buildings where perfect suits are lovingly crafted. **Gieves and Hawkes** *(No. 1)*, tailors since 1771, dressed the explorer Robert Scott and writer Noel Coward. Or you can follow in the footsteps of style icons Fred Astaire and Marlene Dietrich and visit **Anderson**

& Sheppard, around the corner on Old Burlington Street *(No. 32)*. The daddy of them all is **Henry Poole & Co.** *(No. 15)*, the first tailor to set up shop in "The Row" in 1822. Charles Dickens and Napoleon III were customers.

Tube: Piccadilly • savilerowbespoke.com

■ Fortnum & Mason
The finest grocery store in the neighborhood sells wines produced only for Fortnum's and honey from its rooftop apiary. Treat yourself to a pot of Fortnum Pickle or a packet of Chocolossus Biscuits. Then relax over afternoon tea.

181 Piccadilly, W1 • tel 020 7734 8040
Tube: Piccadilly • fortnumandmason.com

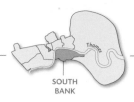

SOUTH
BANK

South Bank

Soar above the city on the stratospheric wheel of the London Eye, then stroll from Westminster Bridge to Tower Bridge to enjoy a nearly limitless supply of free entertainment. Attend a festival, listen to live music, jog, cycle, skateboard, or simply walk along the 3-mile (4.8 km) riverfront. Step into the free Tate Modern art gallery, worth visiting as much for the architecture and the views from the cafe as for the art inside. Paying attractions include a cluster of cultural centers around Waterloo Bridge, housing the Southbank Centre's concert halls, the National Theatre, and the British Film Institute. Travel back in time at the rebuilt Globe theater, where you can see plays performed as they were in Shakespeare's time. Continue east, stopping to admire a replica of the ship that took Sir Francis Drake around the world. Nearby Clink Prison is not for the fainthearted. Foodies will find delights aplenty at Borough Market's al fresco stalls, while the restaurants of Butler's Wharf just east of Tower Bridge serve up pricier fare in more formal surroundings.

❶ **Traveling at a gentle speed of about 10 inches (25 cm) per second, the London Eye carries you far above the capital.**

NEIGHBORHOOD **WALK**

South Bank

Promenade along this section of the Thames to catch the best river views.
Stop for lunch or a snack, then take in an art show or concert.

SOUTH BANK

❹ National Theatre (see p. 75) **In summer catch a performance in front of the building, then stroll east toward the Millennium Bridge.**

❺ Tate Modern (see pp. 78–79) **Art created since 1900 occupies this former power station. Continue east alongside the river.**

❸ Southbank Centre (see pp. 74–75) **Visit London's leading arts center for an art show or a performance before continuing on under Waterloo Bridge.**

❷ London Eye (see p. 74) Float upward on this giant wheel for the best views of the city. Next, walk northeast along the river for about five minutes.

❶ Imperial War Museum (see p. 74) After exploring the collection of arms and weapons, head northwest toward Westminster Bridge, then take the steps on the right just before the bridge.

SOUTHBANK DISTANCE: 3.5 MILES (5.4 KM)
TIME: APPROX. 4–6 HOURS TUBE START: LAMBETH NORTH

72 | WALKING LONDON

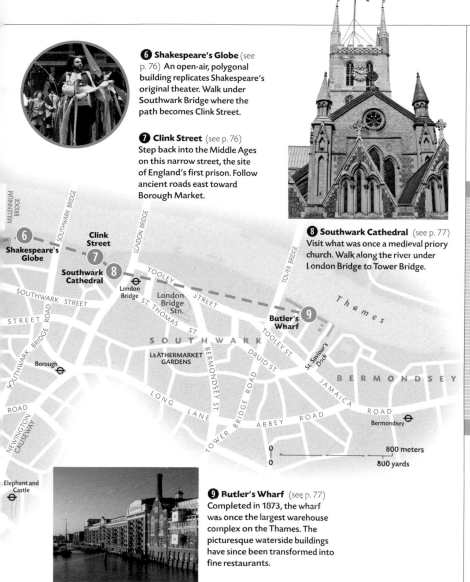

6 Shakespeare's Globe (see p. 76) An open-air, polygonal building replicates Shakespeare's original theater. Walk under Southwark Bridge where the path becomes Clink Street.

7 Clink Street (see p. 76) Step back into the Middle Ages on this narrow street, the site of England's first prison. Follow ancient roads east toward Borough Market.

8 Southwark Cathedral (see p. 77) Visit what was once a medieval priory church. Walk along the river under London Bridge to Tower Bridge.

9 Butler's Wharf (see p. 77) Completed in 1873, the wharf was once the largest warehouse complex on the Thames. The picturesque waterside buildings have since been transformed into fine restaurants.

Imperial War Museum

1 Rockets, tanks, and fighter aircraft vie for the visitor's attention, but it is the **First World War Experience,** a major permanent exhibition that opened on the centenary of the start of the war, that is most compelling. World War II and the impact of the Blitz on London also stand out, and there is a moving section on the Holocaust. A major collection of war art includes drawings, watercolors, and oils by Paul Nash and work by Henry Moore.

Lambeth Road, SE1 • tel 020 7416 5000 • Closed Dec. 24–26 • Tube: Lambeth North • iwm.org.uk

SAVVY **TRAVELER**

Book a "flight" on the London Eye online to get a discount and avoid the lines, which can be lengthy, especially in summer. The ticket office is next to the London Eye, in County Hall, former home of London's local government. County Hall now also houses **Namco Funscape,** a palace of games, bumper cars, and bowling. The **Sea Life London Aquarium** is here, too, showing marine life over three floors and offering the chance to snorkel with sharks.

London Eye

2 Adding its own distinctive silhouette to the London skyline, the Eye, at 443 feet (135 m) high, is the world's tallest cantilevered observation wheel. The gentle ascent in one of its pods reveals glorious views across the capital, from the Houses of Parliament, almost below, in a 25-mile (40 km) sweep south to the North Downs hills, east to Elizabeth II Bridge, and west to Windsor Castle.

Riverside Building, County Hall, Westminster Bridge, SE1 • tel 0871 781 3000 • Closed Dec. 25 • £££££ • Tube: Waterloo, Embankment, or Westminster • londoneye.com

Southbank Centre

3 At the heart of the South Bank's buzzing arts complex lies the **Royal Festival Hall,** which opened in 1951 as part of the Festival of Britain to bolster spirits (and business) after World War II. It is home to four resident orchestras, including the London Philharmonic and London Sinfonietta, while smaller ensembles perform at the adjacent **Queen Elizabeth Hall** and **Purcell Room.** The Festival Hall's main bar and **Clore Ballroom** often offer free live music, while the

SOUTH BANK

A World War II British Spitfire plane and a German V2 Rocket in the Imperial War Museum.

riverside terrace is ideal for people-watching. The **Hayward Gallery** hosts contemporary art shows, and children will love the cartoons on touch-sensitive monitors in the **Waterloo Sunset Pavilion.** The neighboring **BFI Southbank** screens movies old and new and runs film festivals. Its IMAX cinema has the largest screen in the UK.

South Bank, SE1 • tel 020 3879 9555 • ££–£££££ • Tube: Embankment or Waterloo • southbankcentre.co.uk

National Theatre

4 Opened in 1976, the "NT" stages more than a thousand performances of classical and contemporary drama annually in its three theaters. You can also attend talks, take backstage tours, listen to live music in the foyers, and enjoy river views from the terraces.

South Bank, SE1 • tel 020 7452 3000 • Box Office closed public holidays • Tube: Embankment or Waterloo • nationaltheatre.org.uk

Tate Modern

5 See pp. 78–79.

Bankside, SE1 • tel 020 7887 8888 • Closed Dec. 24–26 • Tube: Southwark, St. Paul's, or Blackfriars • tate.org.uk

SOUTH BANK

GOOD **EATS**

■ AQUA SHARD
One of several restaurants in Europe's second-tallest building, this one, on Level 31, specializes in modern British cuisine.
32 London Bridge St., SE1, tel 020 3011 1256, £££

■ CONCRETE CAFE
This stylish garden terrace bar and café atop Queen Elizabeth Hall is a great place to stop for a bite and a drink.
Belvedere Road, SE1, tel 020 7921 0758, £

■ TAS PIDE
This attractive wood-beamed Turkish restaurant serves boat-shaped *pide,* a kind of pizza, along with other tasty Anatolian dishes, both meat and vegetarian.
20 New Globe Walk, SE1, tel 020 7928 3300, £–££

Shakespeare's Globe

6 This wonderful reconstruction of William Shakespeare's open-air theater transports visitors back to the turn of the 17th century. Audiences see the play as a late-Elizabethan audience would have, either seated or as "groundlings," standing around the stage. The season starts on Shakespeare's birthday (April 23). Visit the exhibition or book a candlelit performance at the rebuilt Jacobean **Sam Wanamaker Playhouse,** the most recent addition to this site.

21 New Globe Walk, SE1 • tel 020 7401 9919 • Performances daily Apr. 23–early Oct. • Tube: London Bridge • shakespearesglobe.com

Clink Street

7 Clink Street runs between the riverside Anchor Pub and **St. Mary Overie's Dock,** where you can see a full-scale working replica of Sir Francis Drake's ship, *The Golden Hinde,* in which he circumnavigated the globe in 1577–1580. This narrow street is named for England's first prison, set up in a cellar of the Bishop of Winchester's Palace in 1150. You can still see the west wall and rose window of the palace's Great Hall from the street. **The Clink Prison Museum,** on the site of the original jail, offers insights into crime and punishment and has a worn execution block on show.

Clink St., SE1 • *The Golden Hinde*: tel 020 7403 0123, closed Dec. 24–25, ££, goldenhinde.co.uk • The Clink Prison Museum: tel 020 7403 0900, closed Dec. 25, ££-£££, clink.co.uk • Tube: London Bridge

Southwark Cathedral

8 This elegant, historic building served as a church for a medieval Augustinian monastery before becoming a cathedral in 1905, when it was refurbished. Its many interesting wood carvings include a 13th-century effigy of a recumbent knight and the **Great Screen** behind the altar, installed in 1520. The **Harvard Chapel** reminds visitors that John Harvard, founder of Harvard University, was baptized here in 1607. In the choir, the **Humble Monument** to merchant Richard Humble was carved circa 1616 by a group of Flemish refugee sculptors who belonged to the Southwark School of stonemasons. The church's theater connections date from Elizabethan times and are attested in the nave by a much later stained-glass window (1954) and statue (1912) to Shakespeare—whose spring birthday is celebrated here annually—and a memorial to American actor and director Sam Wanamaker, the driving force behind the rebuilding of the Globe in the 1990s. The cathedral is a popular concert venue, and the churchyard attracts picnickers from the adjacent **Borough Market** (see p. 82).

London Bridge, SE1 • tel 020 7367 6700 • Donations • Tube: London Bridge • cathedral.southwark.anglican.org

Butler's Wharf

9 A wander along Shad Thames on the east side of **Tower Bridge** brings you to Butler's Wharf and a canyon of renovated, 19th-century brick warehouses. Imagine cargo swinging from cranes or rattling along the cobbled stones on iron-wheeled carts. Butler's Wharf housed the largest tea warehouse in the British Empire, and today tea and much else is sold in the specialist stores here. Enjoy al fresco dining on the promenade in the shadow of Tower Bridge.

High-level walkways across Shad Thames were once used for moving cargo between warehouses.

Butler's Wharf, SE1 • Tube: London Bridge

Tate Modern

*The latest works by contemporary artists join forces
with the nation's collection of 20th-century art.*

Tate Modern occupies the former Bankside power station on the bank of the Thames.

The move to a spacious new riverside location in 2000 allowed the Tate's
modern art collection to be displayed in a new way. Works from the landmark
art movements of the 20th century, including surrealism, abstract
expressionism, and pop art, are grouped thematically to show how they
overlapped with and influenced the work of other artists, and how later
artists, sometimes working in different media, responded to them. The gallery
also shows major loan exhibitions.

TURBINE HALL

Every year the Tate invites an artist of international renown to create an installation in the vast Turbine Hall, greeting visitors as they enter the building. Previous artists have included Louise Bourgeois and Anish Kapoor, so expect the spectacular and thought-provoking.

LEVELS 2, 3, & 4

Each of these three floors has a main gallery at either end of the Turbine Hall, and there are smaller galleries in between. Temporary exhibitions take place in two of the main galleries while the others show thematic exhibitions drawn from the permanent collection.

ART MOVEMENTS

All the main art movements of the 20th century find a place here, from Postimpressionism to surrealism, cubism, and abstract art. Among the highlights are Salvador Dalí's **"Mountain Lake,"** Giorgio de Chirico's **"The Uncertainty of the Poet,"** Georges Braque's **"Bottles and Fishes,"** and Pablo Picasso's **"Three Dancers."** There is sculpture, too, such as Giacometti's **"Walking Woman."**

THE SEAGRAM MURALS

Tate Modern has eight of Mark Rothko's Seagram murals, commissioned for the Four Seasons Restaurant in New York in 1958. These great swaths of warm color create a reflective mood.

CONTEMPORARY ART

This is the place to go to find the avant garde, from Sixties conceptual artist **Joseph Beuys** to video artists **Bill Viola** and **Steve McQueen.**

PERFORMANCE

Tate has a regular program of talks and films on and about artists, and there are occasional performances in the **Turbine Hall**, a vast, iconic space for large-scale sculpture and site-specific installation art.

Bankside, SE1 • tel 020 7887 8888 • Closed Dec. 24–26 • Free except for major loan exhibitions • Tube: Southwark, St. Paul's, or Blackfriars • tate.org.uk/modern

SOUTH BANK

Shakespeare's City

London in the late 16th and early 17th centuries was a colorful, noisy, bustling place. From the monarch to the humblest apprentice, Londoners loved pageantry, music, and spectacle, not only on state occasions but also at the city authorities' brilliant street and river parades. It is no wonder that they embraced the new form of entertainment provided by the theaters and that William Shakespeare, the self-made man of native genius, shot to fame.

Shakespeare's memorial in Southwark Cathedral (above); theatergoers clutch red cushions (right) to pad the Globe's hard wooden seats.

A Captive Audience

When William Shakespeare arrived in London from Stratford-upon-Avon around 1588, he was, knowingly or not, making an astute career move. With a population approaching 200,000, flourishing London was England's biggest city.

Shakespeare Takes the Stage

The Bard emerged from obscurity in 1592, when he is mentioned for the first time as a player and dramatist on the London scene. He was a member of the Chamberlain's Men, a company of actors based at The Theatre in Shoreditch, London's first playhouse. Seven years later they moved south across the river to the new Globe.

The Globe became the largest Elizabethan theater, accommodating audiences 3,000 strong. Open to the elements, it was used only in summer; in winter the company retreated indoors to the Blackfriars Playhouse. Alerted by trumpet calls to the latest production, theatergoers would pay a few coins, collected in a box—hence the modern

SOUTH BANK

term "box office"—and stand at ground level or sit in tiered seats around the stage. Actors might be loudly encouraged or abused, and acrobats and jugglers provided entertainment between acts.

The pace of writing and production was frenetic, and the varied repertoire meant that Shakespeare ventured into lyrical comedies, dark tragedies, and Roman plays. His works for the Chamberlain's Men included the three parts of *Henry VI* and *Richard III*. The company performed regularly for Queen Elizabeth I and later—as the King's Men —for King James I. No plays were attributed to Shakespeare after 1613, and he died at Stratford-upon-Avon in 1616.

THE MODERN
GLOBE THEATRE

Shakespeare's Globe was demolished in 1644 by the Puritans during the English Civil War. Almost 350 years later, the American actor and film director Sam Wanamaker initiated the re-creation of the Globe. The open-air playhouse was built on a site close to the original. Inside are wooden galleries, a platform stage, and a circular pit where the audience stands to watch the play (see p. 76).

(see p. 76)

SOUTH BANK

London's Markets

London has markets for every taste, for connoisseurs, collectors, browsers, fashionistas, and foodies. There are daily street markets, weekly farmers' markets, trendy pop-up markets, and some markets that have existed for many centuries. The best known are hardy perennials.

■ BOROUGH MARKET

More than 130 stalls in this South Bank market sell a mix of artisanal, organic, and local produce. At each one, traders talk passionately about their wares, which include chocolates, home-cured salamis, and raw-milk cheeses. Breathe in mouthwatering smells as you meander from stall to stall, stopping perhaps for grilled Swiss raclette (cheese) slathered over boiled potatoes and gherkins. Or choose a meringue from the top of a crispy tower at one of the many patisseries. Butchers at **The Ginger Pig** offer advice on how to cook their fine meats, and piles of colorful fruit and vegetables catch the eye. Rest your legs at **Maria's Market Cafe**—a market institution that serves up baps (soft rolls) filled with meaty delights.

Stoney St., SE1 • tel 020 7407 1002 • Closed Sun. (partial market Mon.-Tue.) • Tube: London Bridge • boroughmarket.org.uk

■ PORTOBELLO ROAD

More than a thousand dealers operate on London's best-known antiques street. The shops, arcades, and galleries that line the street are Aladdin's caves and the Saturday market stalls a visual feast. Find sporting equipment at **Henry Gregory** (*No. 82*), silver in the **Portobello Antique Store** (*No. 79*), and chandeliers at **Judy Fox Antiques** (*No. 81*). The central section, beyond Elgin Crescent, has street food, while **Books for Cooks** (*4 Blenheim Crescent*), on a side street, creates daily lunchtime dishes using the recipes on its shelves. The **Electric Cinema** (*No. 191*), which opened in 1910, is one of the most comfortable movie theaters in London. For retro fashion it is hard to beat **282 Portobello Road** (*No. 282*) or the stalls under Westway flyover.

Portobello Road, W11 • tel 020 7361 3001 • Stalls Sat. only • Tube: Notting Hill Gate or Ladbroke Grove • portobelloroad.co.uk

You can find expert cheesemakers from all over the United Kingdom at Borough Market.

■ BRICK LANE

East London's trendiest street is famous for its curry houses, arts scene, and vintage clothing, but it is particularly popular on Sunday, when it hosts a large and lively market. Vintage is the default style of East London, and this is the place to go for pre-worn and retro fashion, as well as contemporary, often hand-sewn, fashion by young designers. Shoppers pour into **The Old Truman Brewery** (*No. 91*), a huge industrial space crammed with stalls that describes itself as an arts and media quarter.

Its **Sunday Upmarket** sets the style. Musicians and other performers keep the queues that form at **Beigel Bake** (*No. 159*) entertained. Open 24 hours, this East End institution produces more than 7,000 bagels every day (and evening, when it caters to a lively nightlife scene). Street signs around Brick Lane are in Bengali as well as English, reflecting the ethnic origin of the local community, and the kind of food to expect in many of the restaurants.

Shoreditch, E1 • Tube: Aldgate East
• visitbricklane.org

Trafalgar Square & Soho

From the top of his lofty column, Admiral Lord Nelson looks down on the ebbing and flowing crowds in Trafalgar Square as people hurry to other destinations, rest by the fountains, or throng the entrance to the National Gallery on the square's north side. Across the road, the church of St. Martin-in-the-Fields provides an atmospheric setting for candlelight concerts. Leicester Square is the place to see the latest movies or find a theater seat at the half-price ticket booth. Wedged between Leicester Square and the theaters on Shaftesbury Avenue, Chinatown buzzes with Asian restaurants, while European immigrants have brought a continental flavor to Soho, where the sound of jazz spills out of the clubs. All of these destinations are within a stone's throw of each other.

❶ Designed by architect Sir Charles Barry on a site that had been used to stable the monarch's horses, Trafalgar Square took shape in the 1840s.

NEIGHBORHOOD **WALK**

Trafalgar Square & Soho

Stroll through the West End, where theaters, cinemas, and restaurants abound, and feel the excitement of all that the city has to offer.

❾ Soho Square (see p. 91) **The square's gardens, near the lively restaurant area around Frith and Greek Streets, make a pleasant spot for a picnic and to enjoy open-air concerts in summer. Movie companies and advertising agencies surround the square.**

❽ Chinatown (see p. 91) **Revel in one of the liveliest, most colorful areas of the city, bustling with restaurants, food shops, and stalls, then cross back over Shaftesbury Avenue and stroll up Frith Street to Soho Square.**

❼ Shaftesbury Avenue (see pp. 90–91) **Stroll up this street of traditional theaters, where red velvet and golden cherubs encircle boxes rising majestically toward "the gods." Turn south onto Wardour Street and east onto Gerrard Street.**

ST. GILES HIGH ST.

CHARING CROSS ROAD

Tottenham
Court Road

OXFORD STREET

GREEK STREET

FRITH STREET

Soho ⑨
Square

DEAN STREET

S O H O

COMPTON ST

WARDOUR STREET

BERWICK STREET

CARNABY STREET

0 ┣━━━┫ 300 meters
0 ┣━━━┫ 300 yards

6 Leicester Square (see pp. 89–90) **Watch for movie stars' handprints paving the square where major motion pictures premiere. Leave from the northwest corner and stroll along Coventry Street to Piccadilly Circus.**

4 St. Martin-in-the-Fields

5 St. Martin-in-the-Fields (see p. 89) **Step inside this 18th-century church and stay perhaps for a concert or a bite to eat in the café. On leaving, head north on St. Martin's Place and turn left onto Irving Street.**

ST. MARTIN'S LANE

Leicester Square

CHARING CROSS ROAD

ST. MARTIN'S PL.

STRAND

DUNCANNON ST.

Charing Cross

Leicester Square

IRVING ST.

3 National Portrait Gallery

2 National Gallery

1 Trafalgar Square

COCKSPUR ST.

ORANGE ST.

1 Trafalgar Square (see p. 88) **Begin where all London meets, by the fountains beneath Nelson's Column, then cross the square to the National Gallery on the north side.**

2 National Gallery (see pp. 92–93) **Check out one of the world's most impressive collections of Western European art. Outside, turn left and go around the side to St. Martin's Place.**

3 National Portrait Gallery (see p. 88) **From kings and queens to politicians and pop stars, this is where you can put faces to familiar names, then cross St. Martin's Place to St. Martin-in-the-Fields.**

8 Chinatown

GERRARD ST.

LISLE ST.

Pedestrian streets

AVENUE

7 Shaftesbury Avenue

SHAFTESBURY

BREWER ST.

GOLDEN SQUARE

HAYMARKET

Piccadilly Circus

6 Piccadilly Circus - Eros

7 Piccadilly Circus (see p. 90) **Pause to view the statue of Eros in Piccadilly Circus, the symbol of London's West End—a changing area of constant amusement— then turn up Shaftesbury Avenue.**

TRAFALGAR SQUARE & SOHO DISTANCE: 2 MILES (3.2 KM)
TIME: APPROX. 6–8 HOURS TUBE START: CHARING CROSS

Trafalgar Square

1 Admiral Horatio Lord Nelson was cut down at the moment of victory in the naval battle off Cape Trafalgar in southwest Spain in 1805, while engaging the combined Spanish and French fleets of Napoleon Bonaparte. Glory lives on in the square, a place of enjoyment for all Londoners and a frequent focus for rallies and demonstrations, festivals, and concerts.

Nelson's Column, designed by William Railton, was erected in 1843. Four lions by the Victorian artist Sir Edwin Landseer guard the column, and friezes illustrating Nelson's sea victories, cast in bronze from captured cannon, decorate the base. The **Fourth Plinth,** in the square's northwest corner, features a changing exhibit of contemporary art.

IN **THE KNOW**

Nelson's Column stands 170 feet (52 m) high, including the hero's figure at 18 feet (5.5 m) tall. The top of the column on which the statue rests is so large it is said that, when it was erected, a dining table was placed on it and 14 stonemasons sat down to eat.

Intersection of Charing Cross Rd. and the Strand • Tube: Charing Cross or Embankment • london.gov.uk/trafalgarsquare

National Gallery

2 See pp. 92–93.

Trafalgar Sq., WC2 • tel 020 7747 2885 • Closed Jan. 1 and Dec. 24–26 • Temporary exhibitions: £££ • Tube: Charing Cross or Leicester Square • nationalgallery.org.uk

National Portrait Gallery

3 Studies of famous living people and heroes from British history, politics, sports, and the arts feature among the gallery's ever-expanding showcase. Seek out Marcus Gheeraerts's painting of the richly attired Queen Elizabeth I, and don't miss the only known contemporary portrait of playwright William Shakespeare. The ground floor shows an eclectic selection of 21st-century figures.

St. Martin's Pl., WC2 • tel 020 7306 0055 • Closed Dec. 24–26 • Temporary exhibitions: £££ • Tube: Charing Cross or Leicester Square • npg.org.uk

The National Gallery, left, and St. Martin-in-the-Fields, center, overlook Trafalgar Square.

St. Martin-in-the-Fields

4 Built by James Gibbs in 1726, this royal church has been much copied, especially in New England. The royal coat of arms above the entrance indicates that it is the parish church for Buckingham Palace—you can see the royal box on the left as you enter. Known for its music, the church hosts regular concerts. The **Café in the Crypt** (see p. 90) pulsates to jazz on Wednesday nights.

Trafalgar Sq., WC2 • tel 020 7766 1100 • Free concerts Mon., Wed., & Fri. at 1 p.m. • Tube: Charing Cross • stmartin-in-the-fields.org

Leicester Square

5 The red carpets are rolled out here for movie premieres, in keeping with the square's long history as a place of entertainment. On the north side, the **Empire** and **Hippodrome,** both now with casinos, were once music halls. London-born

Charlie Chaplin appeared at the Hippodrome, and a statue of him stands in Leicester Place. William Shakespeare's fountain graces the central square, which is locked at night. The half-price ticket booth, tkts *(tkts.co.uk)* is the place to come for same-day theater tickets, which are sold beginning at 10 a.m.

Between Coventry St., W1, and Cranbourn St., WC2 • Tube: Leicester Square or Piccadilly Circus • leicestersquare.london

TRAFALGAR SQUARE & SOHO

GOOD **EATS**

■ **CAFÉ IN THE CRYPT**
A Londoners' favorite below St. Martin-in-the-Fields, serving hot and cold dishes. Bread-and-butter pudding with a topping of custard is a specialty.
**Trafalgar Sq., WC2,
tel 020 7766 1158, £**

■ **PATISSERIE VALERIE**
Sample cake-making as an art form in this long-established café or snack on scrambled eggs and quiche.
**44 Old Compton St., W1,
tel 020 7437 3466, ££**

■ **PORTRAIT BAR AND RESTAURANT**
Have breakfast, lunch, or tea at the top of the National Portrait Gallery while enjoying a bird's-eye view of Trafalgar Square.
**St. Martin's Pl., WC2,
tel 020 7312 2490, ££££**

Piccadilly Circus

6 A few steps west of Leicester Square, the figure of **Eros,** erected in Piccadilly in 1893, marks the heart of the West End's theaterland. Around this timeless statue, ever-changing entertainment venues come and go. The sites of the former London Pavilion music hall and neighboring onetime Palace of Varieties have kept their facades among modern souvenir shops and garish neon lights. Still functioning are the **Criterion Theatre** *(2 Jermyn St., W1, tel 0844 815 6131)*, which lies below ground, and the adjoining Granaio restaurant *(224 Piccadilly, W1, tel 020 7930 1459, ££££)* is a visual treat. And a Coca-Cola advertisement has beamed across the square since 1955—now incorporated in a state-of-the-art interactive LED screen.

Intersection of Piccadilly and Regent St. , W1 • Tube: Piccadilly Circus

Shaftesbury Avenue

7 Philanthropist Anthony Lord Shaftesbury cleared slums in the 1880s to create Shaftesbury Avenue, running northeast from Piccadilly Circus. Many West End theaters have congregated here. All exude Edwardian grandeur—take a peek at their foyers. **The Lyric** *(No. 29)* is the oldest, built in 1888; the **Apollo**

(No. 31) houses the steepest upper gallery in London. The two giants, both seating around 1,400 and dating from 1911, are the **Palace Theatre** *(No. 109)* and the **Shaftesbury** *(No. 210)*. Built as the Royal English Opera House, the Palace has long been popular for musicals—*Les Misérables* ran here for 18 years—while the Shaftesbury throbbed to the 1960s hit, *Hair*.

Tube: Piccadilly Circus, Leicester Square, or Tottenham Court Road
• londontheatredirect.com

Chinatown

8 On Sundays, St. Martin-in-the-Fields (see p. 89) holds services in Cantonese and Mandarin for the local Chinese population. Red-and-gold gateways herald the way to a collection of pedestrian streets based around **Gerrard Street** on the south side of Shaftesbury Avenue. More than 70 restaurants, serving Cantonese, Szechuan, Japanese, Thai, and Malaysian foods, among others, provide ample choice. Have a specialty tea in Jen Café *(4–8 Newport Pl., WC2, ££)*, where you can see dumplings being rolled in the window. Always lively, Chinatown explodes with excitement during Chinese New Year (late January or early February).

Intersection of Shaftesbury Ave. and Whitcomb St., W1
• Tube: Leicester Square, Piccadilly Circus, or Tottenham Court Road • chinatown.co.uk

Soho Square

9 Workers and shoppers alike are drawn to the attractive garden in Soho Square, a summer venue for free concerts and festivals. The **statue of King Charles II** is a reminder that the square was once called King's Square and was one of the most fashionable addresses in town. Today it lies at the heart of the U.K.'s film industry.

More than 50 shops serving the needs of London's Chinese community cluster in and around Gerrard Street.

Intersection of Greek St. and Sutton Row, W1
• Tube: Piccadilly Circus or Tottenham Court Road

National Gallery

Founded in 1824, the national collection of Western European painting contains a rich and varied range of works by the great masters.

The National Gallery's collection comprises more than 2,300 works of art.

The National Gallery houses one of the world's great art collections, tracing the story of Western European painting from the early 13th century to the turn of the 20th. The collection is arranged chronologically, starting with the early Renaissance galleries in the Sainsbury Wing, continuing in the main building with the great masters of the 16th to 19th centuries, and ending with the Postimpressionists. Free admission to the permanent collection underpins the gallery's founding principle of "art for all."

■ FAVORITE SCENES

Start in the newest part of the gallery, the Sainsbury Wing, where the oldest paintings in the collection hang. During the early Renaissance (13th–15th centuries) most paintings had religious subjects, but portraits and scenes from history were also popular. Check out **"The Arnolfini Portrait"** (Room 56) by Van Eyck, an early master of oil painting, and Piero's **"Baptism of Christ"** (Room 66), set in a Tuscan landscape.

■ CARTOONS & MYSTERIES

Walk through to the main building's West Wing, where the story of the Renaissance continues. Among the star exhibits are Leonardo da Vinci's cartoon (drawing) of the **"Virgin and Child"** (Room 51). If you enjoy mysteries, look at Hans Holbein's **"The Ambassadors"** (Room 4). This portrait of two young men also contains a distorted skull, provoking much debate about its meaning.

■ COURT TO COUNTRY

The rooms in the North Wing introduce Dutch and French artists from the 17th century. A highlight

SAVVY **TRAVELER**

Check out the gallery's varied program of events, including guided tours, talks, concerts, and family workshops during school vacations. There are free weekday talks at lunchtime and in the afternoons. On Friday evenings, the doors stay open until 9 p.m., and often you can stroll through the rooms to the sound of live music.

among London court painter Anthony van Dyck's works is **"Equestrian Portrait of Charles I"** (Room 31).

For 19th-century British painting don't miss Room 34 in the East Wing. Masterpieces on show include John Constable's landscape **"The Hay Wain"** and J. M. W. Turner's ethereal **"Rain, Steam, and Speed."**

■ IMPRESSIONISM & POSTIMPRESSIONISM

Among the Impressionists, Claude Monet is well represented—seek out **"Bathers at La Grenouillère"** (Room 43) from 1869. Postimpressionist Paul Cézanne's **"Bathers"** hangs in Room 45. In the same room you can see **"Chair,"** **"Sunflowers,"** and **"A Wheatfield, with Cypresses,"** all by Vincent van Gogh.

TRAFALGAR SQUARE & SOHO

Trafalgar Sq., WC2 • tel 020 7747 2885 • Closed Jan. 1 and Dec. 24–26 • Temporary exhibitions: £££ • Tube: Charing Cross or Leicester Square • nationalgallery.org.uk

Pub Culture

Inns, taverns, and alehouses—the forerunners of today's pubs—have been part of the London scene for hundreds of years. You can spot a pub—short for "public house"—by its artistic signage and often quaint exterior. Here, as long ago, travelers find refreshment, workers take time out, and friends relax together. Order a "pint of bitter," the traditional tipple, from the bar or choose from a multitude of other beverages.

Many old pubs, like Ye Olde Cheshire Cheese (above), have small, cozy bars; a refreshing pint of chilled lager (right).

Monks & Medieval Inns

The pub has its roots in the inns, taverns, and alehouses of medieval London. Of these, the Tabard Inn in Southwark was immortalized in literature. There, the 14th-century poet Geoffrey Chaucer's pilgrims gathered at the start of *The Canterbury Tales*. As with many such places, it had monastic associations. Its founder was an abbot, who wanted a base when he or his monks came up to the capital. You can still refresh yourself at its close neighbor, **The George** (*77 Borough High St., SE1, tel 020 7407 2056*), a galleried coaching inn.

Home Brew

In medieval times, inns such as the Tabard and George provided food, drink, and beds for wealthy wayfarers. Taverns offered food washed down with wine, while alehouses served ale and simple fare for poorer people. Many alehouses were run by women, who made ale for their families, as it was safer to drink than city water. In 1500, the introduction of the tangy-flavored hop from Germany, which produced a longer-lasting beer, heralded the arrival of specialized breweries, and alehouses became more sophisticated.

Glitzy Decor

In the 17th century, Londoners developed a taste for cheap gin, which by the 19th century was being served in "gin palaces." These premises offered unheard-of luxuries to working-class Londoners—plate-glass windows, mirrors, and gas lighting. Pubs (as alehouses and inns were becoming known) followed suit with new premises, such as the **Princess Louise** (*208 High Holborn, WC1, tel 020 7405 8816*), built in 1872. The late 19th century brought a boom in pub building; no new suburb was complete without its parish church and its pub.

ALL IN **A NAME**

Pub names often tell a story. Several are called The Marquis of Granby after a general in the 1700s who paid to set up wounded soldiers as pub-keepers. Crossed Keys are named for St. Peter, who was said to hold the keys to heaven. Red Lions, heraldic symbol of Scotland, hark back to the coronation of King James VI of Scotland as James I of England. And Bears would have held bear-baiting events.

Gourmet Eating

There is no shortage of fine-dining opportunities in London, a city replete with more than 70 Michelin-starred restaurants. Visiting foodies can sample outstanding cuisine, crafted by top-name chefs and their award-winning protégés. Modern British, gourmet French, light Italian—the choice is yours.

■ SOHO
Once called London's larder, Soho was the birthplace of the city's gourmet restaurant scene, and it is still home to some of the original restaurants. **Quo Vadis** *(26–29 Dean St., W1, tel 020 7437 9585, ££–££££)*, which opened in 1926, excels at modern British cuisine served in its elegant rooms. For celebrity-spotting try **The Ivy** *(1–5 West St., WC2, tel 020 7836 4751, £££–£££££)*, established in Covent Garden in 1917, which serves an updated version of an Edwardian chophouse menu. **Bob Bob Ricard** *(1 Upper James St., W1, tel 020 3145 1000, £££££)* is one of the starriest settings for dining, with brass "press for Champagne" buttons at each table.

■ A SOURCE OF INSPIRATION
One of London's most influential restaurants was opened in Mayfair in 1967 by the Roux family. **Le Gavroche** *(43 Upper Brook St., W1, tel 020 7408 0881, £££££)* was the U.K.'s first restaurant to be awarded three Michelin stars (although later reduced to two). Chefs such as Marco Pierre White and Gordon Ramsay worked here before going on to have glittering careers of their own. In the 1980s, Fulham's **River Café** *(Thames Wharf, Rainville Rd., W6, tel 020 7386 4200, £££££)* and Chelsea's **Bibendum** *(Michelin House, 81 Fulham Rd., SW3, tel 020 7581 5817, £££££)* introduced modern takes on Italian and French cuisine, respectively.

■ HIGH-END HOTEL DINING
Recent years have seen a boom in gourmet dining at London's upscale hotels. Top of anyone's list, with a three-month waiting list, is Heston Blumenthal's **Dinner** *(66 Knightsbridge, SW1, tel 020 7201 3833, £££££)* at the Mandarin

The Italian menu changes twice daily at the River Café, on the banks of the Thames at Fulham.

Oriental, near Harrods. The celebrity chef's unique approach to cooking includes fresh interpretations of historic dishes, such as Powdered Duck (the dish originated in around 1670). For fabulous French fare, head to Mayfair and **Hélène Darroze at The Connaught** (*Carlos Pl., W1, tel 020 3147 7200, £££££*) or **Alain Ducasse** (*Park Lane, W1, tel 020 7629 8866, £££££*) at the Dorchester, or to Knightsbridge and Michelin-starred **Markus** (*Wilton Pl., SW1, tel 020 7235 1200, £££–£££££*) at the Berkeley, which offer seasonal modern English dishes. **Davies & Brook** (*Brook St.,*

W1, tel 020 7629 8860, £££££) at Claridge's offers chef Dmitri Magi's exceptional fare.

■ THE NEXT GENERATION
For a less formal outing, watch for places run by young chefs who have trained at the city's great restaurants. Anna Hansen runs **The Modern Pantry** (*48 St. John's Sq., EC1, tel 020 7553 9210, ££££*) in Clerkenwell, offering a fresh approach on an East-meets-West theme. Joseph Fox's **The Petersham** (*2 Floral Ct., Covent Garden, WC2, tel 020 7305 7676, £££*) offers Italian flavors in gorgeous garden surrounds.

Covent Garden to Ludgate Hill

The north bank of the Thames between Trafalgar Square and St. Paul's Cathedral on Ludgate Hill holds a warren of streets and alleys with a varied history. Given the raucous street performers and the mass of humanity that swirls through on a daily basis, it is hard to imagine that much of this area was once a tranquil "convent" garden tended by the monks of Westminster Abbey. Confiscated by the Crown during King Henry VIII's dissolution of the monasteries in the 1530s, Covent Garden later became a posh residential quarter. By Victorian times it was a thriving market, while the surrounding area included the hub of London's theater world, hangouts for writers, and the heart of Britain's legal system. Nowadays, the area is also notable for good eating and entertainment.

❶ **The market in Covent Garden provides a mix of shopping, relaxation, and refreshment.**

Covent Garden to Ludgate Hill

Opera and street performance rub shoulders with the British legal system in this area of broad streets and narrow alleys.

❶ **Covent Garden** (see p. 102) Good eats and great entertainment are the hallmarks of this former fruit, vegetable, and flower market. Walk to the west side of the Piazza.

❷ **St. Paul's Covent Garden** (see p. 102) The "Actor's Church" hosts religious services and a wide array of live entertainment, and has a great garden out back. Exit the Piazza's north side (James Street), turn right onto Floral Street, and then walk one block.

❸ **Royal Opera House** (see pp. 102–103) Home to Britain's premier opera and ballet companies, the theater boasts 300 years of performance history. Walk two blocks down Bow Street and right onto Tavistock Street.

❹ **London Transport Museum** (see p. 103) Learn about the world's first subway system, how the city kept moving during the Blitz, and other fascinating facts about London's transportation history. Walk two blocks down Burleigh Street and right onto the Strand.

THEOBALD'S ROAD

PROCTER ST.

HIGH HOLBORN

Holborn

Sir John Soane's Museum
❽

LINCOLN'S INN FIELDS

KINGSWAY

GREAT QUEEN ST.

ENDELL STREET

SHAFTESBURY AVE.

MONMOUTH ST.

C O V E N T
G A R D E N

FLORAL STREET

Royal Opera House

Covent Garden

BOW STREET

ALDWYCH

❸

London Transport Museum

LONG ACRE

St. Paul's Covent Garden ❷

❶

Covent Garden Market

❹

❺ **Strand**

Courtauld Institute & Somerset House ❻

ST. MARTIN'S LANE

EMBANKMENT

STRAND

VICTORIA EMBANKMENT GARDENS

VICTORIA

Charing Cross

Charing Cross Station

Embankment

Embankment Pier

NORTHUMBERLAND AVE.

WATERLOO BRIDGE

(HUNGERFORD) GOLDEN JUBILEE BRIDGES

**COVENT GARDEN TO LUDGATE HILL   DISTANCE: 2 MILES (3.2 KM)
TIME: APPROX. 6–8 HOURS   TUBE START: COVENT GARDEN**

9 St. Bride's Church (see p. 105) Fleet Street's patron church features Wren's "wedding cake" steeple and a crypt displaying archaeological remains from 2,000 years of history.

8 Sir John Soane's Museum (see pp. 104–105) Rather like a miniature version of the British Museum, this was once the home of eccentric architect John Soane and his marvelous collections. Retrace your steps to the front of the Royal Courts. Turn left onto Fleet Street.

7 Royal Courts of Justice (see p. 104) London's legal eagles flock to a Gothic maze that is every bit as complicated as the laws that are enforced within. Follow Bell Yard, then Carey and Serle Streets to Lincoln's Inn Fields behind the R.C.J.

5 Strand (see pp. 103–104) This former Roman road along the northern shore of the Thames was later the haunt of actors, writers, and aristocrats. At Charing Cross, turn right onto Villiers Street.

6 Victoria Embankment (see pp. 106–107) Arcing along the north bank of the Thames between Charing Cross and Temple, this riverside promenade is crammed with intriguing sites. Walk east and turn left on Middle Temple Lane and left on Fleet Street.

Covent Garden

1 Master architect Inigo Jones designed the elegant **Piazza** and its colonnaded buildings in the 1630s as an aristocratic enclave. The square also attracted vendors hawking wares to the rich—a tiny seed of commerce that eventually bloomed into London's primary vegetable, fruit, and flower market. The market pavilion is late Georgian (1830), but for the most part Jones would still recognize the lovely square that he laid out nearly 400 years ago. Covent Garden's evolution into an energetic dining and entertainment hub began in the 1970s, when the food and flower markets moved south of the Thames. Although it looks chaotic at first glance, the **street theater** is carefully orchestrated: Musicians, acrobats, and other buskers must audition for a license to perform in the Piazza, and many have been playing Covent Garden for years.

Covent Garden Piazza, WC2 • Tube: Covent Garden, Leicester Square, or Charing Cross • coventgarden.london

St. Paul's Covent Garden

2 Called the "Actor's Church" because of its affiliation with the local theater world, St. Paul's is another Inigo Jones creation. The facade and its husky Tuscan columns feature in the first scene of George Bernard Shaw's *Pygmalion*, the play that introduced Covent Garden flowergirl Eliza Doolittle. Inside, look out for the plaques commemorating **Vivien Leigh, Charlie Chaplin,** and **Boris Karloff.** Little known to the milling hordes out front, the church's **back garden** is a peaceful oasis amid the hubbub of central London.

Bedford St., WC2 • tel 020 7836 5221• Tube: Covent Garden • actorschurch.org

Royal Opera House

3 From the composer George Frideric Handel and the actor Edmund Kean to the opera singer Jenny Lind and the ballerina Margot Fonteyn, countless great names of stage, music, and dance have played this legendary theater on the northeastern edge of

Covent Garden. The present building (opened in 1858) is the third on the site; fire destroyed the first two. The elegant Corinthian portico fronts a massive auditorium that can seat more than 2,200 patrons for performances by the Royal Opera and Royal Ballet. A program of exhibitions celebrates past productions and visiting companies.

Bow St., WC2 • tel 020 7304 4000 • Tours £££–££££ depending on the tour • Tube: Covent Garden • roh.org.uk

London Transport Museum

4 This museum on the southeast side of Covent Garden tracks 200 years of London's urban transport. Its vast interior (once a flower market) brims, like a Matchbox collection gone mad, with old taxis, trams, Tube cars, carriages, and double-decker buses. Highlights include an old horse-drawn bus, an 1866 steam engine, and an early motor bus. Vintage posters and uniforms complement the vehicles.

Visitors to the Royal Opera House sip Champagne in the ornate iron-and-glass Paul Hamlyn Hall, formerly part of the flower market.

Covent Garden Piazza, WC2 • tel 0343 222 5000 • £££££ • Tube: Covent Garden • ltmuseum.co.uk

The Strand

5 Running 0.75 of a mile (1 km) between Trafalgar Square and Fleet Street, the Strand is one of London's most storied thoroughfares. As the name implies, this was once the north bank of the Thames. It has been a roadway since Roman times, and during the Middle Ages it was lined with palaces. By the Victorian era, it had morphed into a theater hub and literary hangout for the likes of Charles Dickens. Flanked by the **Royal Courts of Justice** (see p. 104) and, at its eastern end, the **Inns of Court** (see pp. 108–109), the street remains the nucleus of London's legal world, while the posh **Savoy Hotel** (1889) is a reminder that Britain's luxury-hotel heritage also began on the Strand. "Islands" in the street host the churches of **St. Mary le Strand** (1717) and **St. Clement Danes** (1681).

Between Trafalgar Sq. and Fleet St. • Tube: Charing Cross or Embankment

Victoria Embankment

6 See pp. 106–107.

Victoria Embankment • Tube: Charing Cross, Embankment, or Temple

GOOD **EATS**

■ **INDIGO**
Stylish modern decor and cutting-edge British cuisine make this restaurant inside the One Aldwych hotel one of London's premier taste treats. **1 Aldwych, WC2, tel 020 7300 0400, ££££**

■ **HAWKSMOOR SEVEN DIALS**
Straightforward and generously sized charcoal grilled steaks or burgers are among the meaty meals served in this historic old brewery. **11 Langley St., WC2, tel 020 7420 9390, ££££**

■ **MON PLAISIR**
The oldest French restaurant in London, this devotedly Gallic favorite offers predictable yet delicious fare, including de rigueur escargots, and a fantastic wine list. It's just off Seven Dials. **19–21 Monmouth St., WC2, tel 020 7836 7243, £££**

COVENT GARDEN TO LUDGATE HILL

Royal Courts of Justice

7 Clinging to legal traditions that stretch back nearly a thousand years, white-wigged judges and lawyers scurry through the maze of hallways, passages, and rooms that compose the geographic heart of British justice. This neo-Gothic labyrinth was built in the late 19th century, and its 88 courts hear many of the nation's most serious civil cases. The main entrance—more like that of a cathedral than a civic building—leads into a **Great Hall** that measures 80 feet (24 m) in height and 238 feet (72 m) in length. The public can attend most cases.

Strand, WC2 • tel 020 7947 6000 • Advance reservation required for tours • Tube: Temple or Charing Cross • theroyalcourtsofjustice.com

Sir John Soane's Museum

8 A man for all seasons, Georgian-era architect John Soane had a keen eye for collecting and bequeathed this sprawling house with its eclectic contents to the British nation. The collection runs a broad gamut from Egyptian and Roman antiquities to paintings by **Hogarth, Canaletto,** and **Turner,** as well as stained glass, rare books,

In Sir John Soane's picture room, paintings hang on panels that open to reveal more paintings.

timepieces, furniture, Chinese tiles, and odds and ends salvaged from other buildings. Contents aside, the house offers a glimpse of cultured, upper middle-class London life in the early 19th century.

13 Lincoln's Inn Fields, WC2 • tel 020 7405 2107 • Closed Mon. and Tue. • Tours £££ • Tube: Holborn or Chancery Lane • soane.org

St. Bride's Church

9 World War II bombing almost destroyed the patron church of London's newspaper business, but the church was rebuilt to Sir Christopher Wren's original design. A 226-foot (69 m) tiered **"wedding-cake" steeple**—the only part that survived the Blitz—crowns the church. The crypt houses a museum, a collection of historic gravestones, and a rare **iron coffin** designed to thwart grave robbers.

Fleet St., EC4 • tel 020 7427 0133 • Tours ££ • Tube: Temple, Blackfriars, or St. Paul's • www.stbrides.com

Victoria Embankment

Stroll this delightful river-walk, with its peaceful gardens, plethora of eclectic statues and monuments, and truly spectacular views.

Victoria Embankment Gardens with the statue of James Outram

Laid out in the 1860s by engineer Sir Joseph Bazalgette to channel the Thames (and a new sewer system), this elegant riverside promenade is graced by granite walls and peaceful public gardens. Arcing between Charing Cross and the City, with Waterloo Bridge as a radius, the wide sweeping Embankment affords magnificent views of the South Bank and along the river, with the dome of St. Paul to the east and the Houses of Parliament to the west.

■ VICTORIA EMBANKMENT GARDENS
This public park extends east from Villiers Street. Tucked in the northwest corner is the York Watergate, built in 1626 as an entry from the Thames for the Duke of Buckingham, whose palatial York House once stood here. Nearby are a **statue of Scottish poet Robert Burns** and the Imperial Camel Corps Memorial honoring the WWI camel-mounted brigade.

■ CLEOPATRA'S NEEDLE
Piercing the Embankment, this 69-foot (21 m) **granite Egyptian obelisk** inscribed with hieroglyphics was originally erected in Heliopolis around 1450 B.C. Gifted to Britain to commemorate the Battle of Alexandria and Battle of the Nile in 1801, it was brought to England in 1878 following a dramatic voyage regaled in bronze plaques at its base. The needle is flanked by bronze sphinxes, one of which still bears shrapnel wounds from a WWI German bomb dropped in 1917.

■ GRAND EDIFICES
Overlooking the Embankment are the 1933 **art deco Shell Max House,** adorned with the largest clockface in London, and the 1889 Savoy Hotel, gleaming afresh following a recent $220 million face-lift. Beyond Waterloo Bridge is palatial

Somerset House, built 1775–1801 to house the Royal Academy of Arts. Today it hosts contemporary art spaces, including the Courtauld Institute of Art (closed for restoration through 2021).

■ TEMPLE
Beyond Somerset House lies Temple, London' legal district. At Temple Pier you can tour the H.M.S. *Wellington*, a sloop that served as a North Atlantic convoy escort in WWII. Beyond, the National Submarine War Memorial honors submariners killed in WWI and WWII. Across the road, Middle Temple's cobbled lanes are still adorned with gas lamps and barristers' chamber; this area is at the heart of the Inns of Court (see pp. 108–109).

The Egyptian-style sphinx to the east of Cleoptra's Needle

Victoria Embankment • Tube: Charing Cross, Embankment, or Temple

Legal Traditions

Like the monarchy, the British legal system has succeeded in adapting to the modern world while retaining picturesque and archaic customs, dress, and procedures. In central London, the Inns of Court—where many lawyers have their offices—and the Courts themselves are treasuries of history as well as working parts of the contemporary legal system. Their gardens provide some of London's most tranquil green spaces.

The Royal Courts of Justice clock (above); lawyers wearing their ceremonial wigs and robes process into a church service (right).

Inns of Court

All barristers (lawyers who act as advocates in court) in England and Wales must be members of one of four associations known collectively as the Inns of Court. These communities of lawyers established themselves on land between the City of London and Westminster around 700 years ago. Two of the Inns of Court, the Inner Temple and Middle Temple, lie between the Thames and Fleet Street. An easy stroll north from Fleet Street along Chancery Lane leads toward the other two, Lincoln's Inn and Gray's Inn.

Providing everything a group of learned men needed—rooms to live and work in, a hall for dining, a church for prayer, a library for reading, and gardens for rest and relaxation—the Inns of Court are oases of cloistered calm in the city. Their walls enclose courtyards and narrow lanes as well as broad expanses of lawn and flowers. Wandering through the grounds of the Inns, visitors glimpse wigged and gowned lawyers heading from their offices to court, burdened with armfuls of files.

The Inner and Middle Temple are particularly rich in history. The 12th-century **Temple Church** (*Inner Temple Lane, WC2, tel 020 7353 3470, templechurch.com*) has a round nave modeled on the Church of the Holy Sepulchre in Jerusalem. Opposite stands the Tudor **Middle Temple Hall,** where the first performance of Shakespeare's comedy, *Twelfth Night,* took place on Candlemas, February 2, 1602.

The Courts

To see the law in action, just walk a short distance from the Inns of Court to the Royal Courts of Justice on the Strand (see p. 103) to hear civil cases, or to the Central Criminal Court at the **Old Bailey** (*Old Bailey, EC4, tel 020 7192 2739, closed weekends and public holidays, courttribunalfinderservice.gov.uk*) for criminal cases.

FORMER MEMBERS OF THE **INNS OF COURT**

William Penn, founder of Pennsylvania, was a member of Lincoln's Inn.

Five signers of the American Declaration of Independence— Edward Rutledge, Thomas Heyward, Thomas McKean, Thomas Lynch, and Arthur Middleton—were members of the Middle Temple. Another signer, William Paca, was a member of the Inner Temple.

The young Charles Dickens was employed as a clerk in Gray's Inn.

House Museums

Writers, artists, statesmen, scientists—many of the great and good have made their homes in London. Whether filled with priceless art collections or the quotidian objects of everyday existence, these houses provide glimpses into the lives and passions of their famous former occupants.

■ DR. JOHNSON'S HOUSE

Situated in a network of passages north of Fleet Street, 17 Gough Square was built around 1700. Dr. Samuel Johnson lived in the house from 1748 to 1759 and compiled his English dictionary here.

17 Gough Sq., EC4 • tel 020 7353 3745 • Closed Sun. and public holidays • ££ • Tube: Blackfriars, Chancery Lane, or Temple • drjohnsonshouse.org

■ JOHN WESLEY'S HOUSE

Founder of Methodism with his brother Charles, John Wesley built this house and chapel in 1779. See his belongings, and visit his study and prayer room.

49 City Rd., EC1 • tel 020 7253 2262 • Closed Sun. and public holidays • Donations • Tube: Old Street • wesleyschapel.org.uk

■ APSLEY HOUSE

Also known as Number One, London, Apsley House on Hyde Park Corner was designed by Robert Adam between 1771 and 1778. The first Duke of Wellington moved here after his victory over Napoleon at Waterloo in 1815. The art collection includes paintings by Velázquez and Rubens and a nude statue of Napoleon.

149 Piccadilly, W1 • tel 020 7499 5676 • Closed certain days (varies by month), Jan. 1, Dec. 24–26 • £££ • Tube: Hyde Park Corner • english-heritage.org.uk

■ BENJAMIN FRANKLIN HOUSE

This Georgian house off Trafalgar Square is the only surviving home of scientist, philosopher, and American founding father Dr. Benjamin Franklin, who lived here between 1757 and 1775.

36 Craven St., WC2 • tel 020 7839 2006 • Closed Tues. Reservation recommended • ££ • Tube: Charing Cross or Embankment • benjaminfranklinhouse.org

■ FREUD MUSEUM

Having escaped Austria after its annexation by Nazi Germany, Sigmund

In Dennis Severs' House, burning candles suggest that the original occupants are nearby.

Freud moved with his family to Hampstead. Here, you can see the couch used by his patients, his study, and his collection of nearly 2,000 Roman, Greek, Egyptian, and Oriental antiquities.

20 Maresfield Gdns., NW3 • tel 020 7435 2002 • Closed Mon.–Tues. • ££ • Tube: Finchley Road • freud.org.uk

■ LINLEY SAMBOURNE HOUSE
This late Victorian town house in Kensington was the home of *Punch* magazine cartoonist and illustrator Edward Linley Sambourne (1844–1910). The house retains original furniture and other possessions of the Sambourne family, including a notable collection of Chinese porcelain.

18 Stafford Ter., W8 • tel 020 7602 3316 • Tours Wed. , Sat. , Sun. 11:15 a.m. • £££ • Tube: High Street Kensington • rbkc.gov.uk/museums

■ DENNIS SEVERS' HOUSE
Would-be time travelers will delight in this Georgian house on Folgate Street in Spitalfields, East London. Visitors are led in silence through the ten rooms, each decorated in a different historical style.

18 Folgate St., E1 • tel 020 7247 4013 • Tours Sun. noon-4 p.m., Mon. noon–2 p.m., Mon., Wed. and Fri. 5-9 p.m. (reservation required) • £££ • Tube: Liverpool Street • dennissevershouse.co.uk

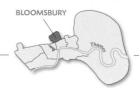

BLOOMSBURY

Bloomsbury

This is the city's intellectual heart, where several colleges of the University of London surround elegant garden squares. Here, in an area loosely bounded by Euston Road to the north and Holborn to the south, are some of the world's foremost repositories of knowledge, including the greatest museum and library in Britain. The architecture is commensurate with this cerebral atmosphere. Stately Georgian town houses mingle with classical churches, imposing art deco office buildings, and a striking neo-Gothic railroad station. In the early 20th century, the Bloomsbury literary set blossomed and revolutionaries espoused new ideologies in this bookish atmosphere. Diplomats have also made their homes here, as many embassies are based in the area. Bloomsbury is not just for the learned elite, however. Peaceful streets offer an oasis of calm. People of all ages will enjoy the old-fashioned playthings at Pollock's Toy Museum.

◐ The more than eight million artifacts in the British Museum's collection include a colossal bust of the Egyptian pharaoh Amenhotep III.

Bloomsbury

*Leafy squares, rows of brick and stone town houses,
and fabulous museums draw visitors to the area.*

7 British Library
(see p. 119) **Every book
you could ever want can
be found here.** Head east
on Euston Road to
St. Pancras International.

5 University College London (see p.
118) Beyond its grandiose neoclassical
facade, London's premier university
is chock-full of museums and sites of
interest. Return to Torrington Place and
turn left to Tavistock Place, then turn
south on Hunter Street.

Euston
Station

Euston

EVERSHOLT STREET

UPPER WOBURN PLACE

EUSTON ROAD

HAMPSTEAD RD.

Euston
Square

EUSTON   ROAD

Warren
Street

GOWER STREET

GORDON
SQUARE

5 University
College London

WOBURN
SQUARE

TOTTENHAM

FITZROY
SQUARE

TORRINGTON

PLACE

COURT

CHENIES ST.

Pollock's
Toy Museum

4 Goodge Street

GOODGE ST.   ROAD

BEDFORD
SQUARE

4 Pollock's Toy Museum
(see p. 117) **Visit this collection
of toys, then return to**
Tottenham Court Road and head
north. Turn east on Torrington
Place then north on Gower Street
to University College London.

Tottenham
Court Road

OXFORD ST.

**BLOOMSBURY DISTANCE: 2.6 MILES (4 KM)
TIME: APPROX. 8 HOURS TUBE START: HOLBORN**

0   400 meters
0   400 yards

8 St. Pancras International
(see p. 119) London's most
appealing rail terminus also likes
to think it is the most romantic.
Relax in the Champagne Bar
or book a room in the newly
restored St. Pancras Renaissance
Hotel.

6 Foundling Museum (see p. 118)
Hundreds of babies were given up to the
Foundling Hospital's care in centuries
past. Head north on Hunter Street to
the British Library.

5 British Museum
(see pp. 120–123) See the mummies and the Elgin
Marbles. Head west to Tottenham Court Road, turn
north and then west onto Goodge Street. Take the
first right, then the first left onto Scala Street.

2 Museum Street (see
p. 116) This short street brims with
interesting shops, galleries, and cafés.
The British Museum is at the north end
of Museum Street.

1 St. George's Church (see p.
116) This recently restored church
has great architectural aspirations.
Turn right onto Museum Street
and head north.

BLOOMSBURY

St. George's Church

1 The final church designed by Sir Christopher Wren's protégé, Nicholas Hawksmoor, was consecrated in 1731 for Bloomsbury's newly established gentry. The church has a portico with Corinthian columns, based on the Roman temple of Bacchus in Baalbec, and the pyramid-like structure on its spire is influenced by Turkey's grand tomb of Mausoleus. The majestically simple interior has been recently restored and is regarded as a high-water mark in the English Baroque style. Its acoustics make it a popular concert venue, and the undercroft holds a permanent exhibition of the church's, and Bloomsbury's, history.

Little Russell St., WC1 • tel 020 7242 1979 • Tube: Holborn • stgeorgesbloomsbury.org.uk

Museum Street

2 Opposite the British Museum is Museum Street—a unique stretch of shops. On the corner is the **Museum Tavern,** whose Victorian interior of mahogany and etched glass is complemented by a range of good British beers. **Abbott and Holder** *(No. 30)* specializes in English paintings, drawings, and prints from the past 250 years. **Atlantis** *(No. 49a)* has been selling occult books since 1922. There are also shops selling reproductions of classical ceramics, statues, and many other interesting items.

Runs from New Oxford St. to Great Russell St. • Tube: Holborn

British Museum

3 See pp. 120–123.

Great Russell St., WC1 • tel 020 7323 8000 • Closed Jan. 1 and Dec. 24–26 • Tube: Tottenham Court Road, Holborn, or Russell Square • britishmuseum.org

GOOD **EATS**

■ **THE LAMB**
Traditional pub-grub and British beer are served in this historic Victorian bar, which has old-style frosted-glass screens for the privacy of the patrons.
**94 Lambs Conduit St., WC1,
tel 020 7405 0713, £**

■ **MARY WARD CENTRE**
This adult education college's vegetarian café and art gallery is a hidden gem. Enjoy great value tasty food in a peaceful Georgian building.
**42 Queen Sq., WC1,
tel 020 7269 6000, £**

■ **PIED À TERRE**
Delicious dishes from seasonal ingredients in a refined atmosphere have earned this restaurant a Michelin star.
**34 Charlotte St., W1,
tel 020 7636 1178, £££££**

BLOOMSBURY

Just west of Museum Street, James Smith & Sons specializes in umbrellas.

Pollock's Toy Museum

4 A clutter of nostalgia—including a **World War I teddy bear** and a **19th-century rocking horse**—fill the rooms of two 18th- and 19th-century houses joined together to form this museum. The collection is based on the work of shopkeeper Benjamin Pollock, who produced toy theaters that could be assembled from sheets of printed card ("a penny plain, tuppence colored"). Pollock's original shop was in Hoxton, East London, and he kept it going from around 1880 until his death in 1937, by which time he was famous for his toys, with such clients as author Robert Louis Stevenson and art critic Serge Diaghilev.

1 Scala St., W1 • tel 020 7636 3452 • Closed Sun. and all public holidays • ££ • Tube: Goodge Street • pollockstoys.com

University College London

5 Founded in 1826, the oldest and largest University of London college boasts Mahatma Gandhi, inventor Alexander Graham

Bell, and comedian Ricky Gervais among its illustrious alumni. The domed Main Building, with its huge neoclassical frontage, is notable for the preserved body of the university's "spiritual founder," philosopher Jeremy Bentham, in a glass case in the South Cloisters. Impressive plaster murals by John Flaxman highlight the UCL Art Museum, which also displays works by Rembrandt, Turner, and Whistler. **The Petrie Museum of Egyptian Archaeology** is a trove of ancient finds, such as sleeved robes and a suit of armor from the time of the pharaohs.

Gower St., WC1 • tel 020 7679 2000 • UCL Art Museum closed Sat.-Mon.; Petrie Museum closed Sun. and Mon. • ucl.ac.uk

Foundling Museum

6 Seventy-five percent of children died before the age of five in mid-18th-century London, and many unwanted babies were abandoned in the street. The philanthropist Capt. Thomas Coram, appalled by such conditions, created the Foundling Hospital in 1739 to take care of the many unwanted babies. They arrived at a rate of around 200 a year, and their mothers often left them with keepsake bows, ribbons, bonnets, and sleeves embroidered with hearts or flowers. A heartrending collection of these mementos is on view. The museum is spread over three floors, displaying period interiors, exhibits of the hospital's history, and an extensive collection of memorabilia of composer George Frideric Handel, who was a benefactor. The large art collection includes paintings by William Hogarth, who also donated money to the hospital. The **Governors' Meeting Room** is described as having London's finest 18th-century rococo interior.

IN **THE KNOW**

Workhouses provided basic but free food and lodging for the poor and unemployed in return for work. They also housed orphaned children.

40 Brunswick Sq., WC1 • tel 020 7841 3600 • Closed Mon. and public holidays • £££ • Tube: Russell Square • foundlingmuseum.org.uk

British Library

7 A copy of every book published in the United Kingdom and the Republic of Ireland is lodged with the British Library, requiring an estimated 6.8 miles (11 km) of new shelf space each year. The building surrounds the **King's Library,** a central glass-walled tower that holds a collection of large leather-bound books amassed by King George III. Although the reading rooms are only for researchers, visitors can enjoy the displays of treasures from the Library's archives, including some of the earliest printed **Shakespeare plays,** original **Beatles lyrics,** and the **Magna Carta,** and listen to historic recordings from the **Sound Archive.**

96 Euston Rd., NW1 • tel 0843 208 1144 • Closed Dec. 25 • Tube: King's Cross St. Pancras • bl.uk

St. Pancras International

8 Completed in 1868, this is a neo-Gothic palace from the age of steam that is now the starting point for the high-speed Eurostar link to the Continent as well as trains to Luton and Gatwick airports. Train travel has always been romantic, and in its refurbished form—columns repainted in their original blue, giving a feeling of open skies—St. Pancras sells itself as a place for courtship. The Champagne Bar, which claims to be Europe's longest, is one possibility. A statue of a kissing couple, titled **"Brief Encounter,"** looms over the concourse. More endearing is the statue of English poet **John Betjeman,** who was a champion of Victorian architecture. Old-world charm is provided at the **St. Pancras Renaissance Hotel** (see p. 185), which opened in the former Midland Grand Hotel, once the most glamorous of London's railway hotels.

Euston Rd., NW1 • tel 020 7843 7688 • Tube: King's Cross St. Pancras • stpancras.com

John Betjeman led a campaign to save St. Pancras in the 1960s.

British Museum

From Egyptian mummies to priceless vases and Aztec masks, London's biggest museum holds some of the world's greatest treasures.

BLOOMSBURY

In the British Museum's Great Court, a café and shops surround the former Reading Room.

It would take weeks to fully explore the 2.5 miles (4 km) of galleries and see even a fraction of the more than eight million ancient and modern objects owned by the British Museum, but it is possible to view the highlights in an hour or two. The majority of the collection of the oldest public museum in the world is displayed on two floors, with most of the galleries in the west wing to the left of the entrance and the larger pieces on the ground floor. Start in the jaw-dropping Great Court to get a sense of the sheer scale of the place.

■ Great Court

The building's heart is the Great Court, designed by architect Norman Foster and opened in 2000. Once an outdoor space around the former Reading Room, it has been enclosed under a lightweight roof to create an indoor public square. There are a dozen ancient statues in the Great Court; the oldest is the head of the **Egyptian pharaoh Amenhotep III,** from around 1350 B.C.

■ The Reading Room

The museum's circular Reading Room opened in 1857. It was here that Karl Marx wrote part of *Das Kapital,* Gandhi studied law, and Sherlock Holmes creator Sir Arthur Conan Doyle and countless other writers researched their books. When the British Library (see p. 119) opened in 1997, the Reading Room closed. Today it is used for temporary exhibits. Look up to admire the blue-and-gold-painted dome, which is made of papier-mâché.

■ Egypt & Near East

Running the length of the western side of the Great Court is the Egyptian Sculpture Gallery (Room 4). Fight your way through the crowds to see the **Rosetta Stone.** This unassuming lump of rock is one

of Egyptology's most prized objects: It provided the key to understanding hieroglyphics. The stone has the same text in hieroglyphics, demotic, and ancient Greek. When it was found in 1799, the ability to read hieroglyphics had been lost for 1,400 years, but two scholars used the ancient Greek text to break the code.

From the Egyptian galleries, the massive human-headed winged bulls from the palace of King Sargon II lead to the Assyrian Galleries (Rooms 6–10). One of the highlights here are **wall reliefs** from the seventh-century B.C. Palace of Nineveh, in modern Iraq, depicting the epic drama of a royal lion hunt (Room 10).

■ Mummies & More

Head upstairs to see more from ancient Egypt (Rooms 61–66), where coffins and mummies—including a **mummified cat** and the **mummy of Katebet,** a woman from Thebes who

BLOOMSBURY

died around 1300–1280 B.C. Katebet was buried wearing a wig, rings on her hands, and a scarab on her stomach that was meant to protect her in the afterlife.

■ GLORIES OF GREECE & ROME
The jewel of the museum's collection are the **Parthenon Sculptures,** known as the **Elgin Marbles** (Room 18). Created for the Parthenon in Athens, these friezes depict the great procession in honor of the goddess Athena, and the struggle between humans and centaurs. Video displays show how the once brightly colored sculptures looked on the outside of the Athenian temple.

The Greek and Roman galleries continue upstairs (Rooms 69–73), with objects from domestic and ceremonial life. Decorated with mythological scenes of love, the blue-and-white Roman cameo-glass **Portland Vase** from around A.D. 525 survived being smashed by a museum visitor in 1845. Glued back together at the time, it was restored in 1987.

■ AMERICA & ASIA
The north side of the Great Court holds objects from the Americas, Asia, and the Islamic world. Artifacts here include a statue from **Easter Island** (Room 24), Native American

The fifth-century B.C. Parthenon Sculptures include dynamic groups of life-size figures.

BLOOMSBURY

headdresses (Room 26), an Aztec **Turquoise Serpent** (Room 27) and masks, as well as jade, ceramics, and items from daily and ritual life.

■ Treasures of Britain
From time to time, Britain yields up its buried treasures—often from graves or underground hiding places. The highlights on display include the greatest Anglo-Saxon treasure trove ever found—the burial hoard from **Sutton Hoo** (Room 41) excavated in 1939, the exquisitely carved **Lewis Chessmen** (Room 40), and **Lindow Man** (Room 50), whose 2,000-year-old body was found almost perfectly preserved in a peat bog. The Sutton Hoo treasure includes a rare helmet decorated with bronze and garnets. The chessmen, which came to light on Scotland's Isle of Lewis in 1831, were carved in Norway of walrus tusks and whale teeth around A.D. 1150.

■ Middle East
In the Middle East galleries (Rooms 52–59), see an example of the world's earliest writing: **Sumerian pictographs** recording trade transactions dating from 3000 B.C.

This helmet from Sutton Hoo was reconstructed from 500 pieces.

The Sumerian Royal Graves of Ur, in modern-day Iraq, date from the mid-third millennium B.C. Many items were buried with the dead, including the **Royal Game of Ur** (Room 56), an ancient board game.

■ Prints & Drawings
The museum has a collection of at least 50,000 drawings and more than two million prints, ranging from Renaissance to modern. Go to Room 90 to see works by Dürer, Michelangelo, Rembrandt, and Goya. The items on show rotate, but there is always something extraordinary to see.

Great Russell St., WC1 • tel 020 7323 8000 • Closed Jan. 1 and Dec. 24–26 • Tube: Tottenham Court Road, Holborn, or Russell Square • britishmuseum.org

BLOOMSBURY

Literary City

Opened in 1857, the British Museum Reading Room (see p. 121) put Bloomsbury at the heart of London's literary scene. Many writers used the room, including revolutionaries Karl Marx and Vladimir Lenin, and authors Charles Dickens and Oscar Wilde. Bloomsbury isn't alone in having a literary history, so look for Blue Plaques—circular blue signs that commemorate the places where famous people lived or worked—on buildings throughout the city.

LITERARY **BLUE PLAQUES**

Agatha Christie,
58 Sheffield Terrace, W8

Daniel Defoe, 95 Stoke
Newington Church St., N16

George Eliot,
31 Wimbledon Park Rd., SW18

Ian Fleming,
22 Ebury St., SW1

Aldous Huxley,
16 Bracknell Gardens, NW3

Henry James,
22 Upper Cheyne Row, SW3

Rudyard Kipling,
43 Villiers St., WC2

Herman Melville,
25 Craven St., WC2

George Orwell,
50 Lawford Rd., NW5

Sylvia Plath,
3 Chalcot Sq., NW1

George Bernard Shaw,
29 Fitzroy Sq., W1

Birthplace of the English Dictionary

When the British Museum first opened, the English language was still being refined. From his home at **17 Gough Square** (see p. 110), Samuel Johnson compiled the first major English dictionary between 1748 and 1759. Despite Johnson's great erudition, some blatant errors still found their way in. When asked why he had defined "pastern" as a horse's knee, rather than its foot, he replied, "ignorance madam, pure ignorance." Yet it was a great success and was considered the preeminent English dictionary for almost 200 years.

Dickensian London

Although William Shakespeare (see pp. 80–81) is lauded as England's greatest writer, Bloomsbury resident Charles Dickens is perhaps the author most associated with London. His novels buzz with the 19th-century city's sights, sounds, smells, landmarks, and teeming crowds of crossing-sweepers, servants, clerks, dressmakers, dancing

BLOOMSBURY

masters, pickpockets, prostitutes, lawyers, ladies, and baronets, all drawn in vivid detail. Many places that today look salubrious have a murky Victorian past, such as Saffron Hill in **Holborn,** where Fagin ran his den of criminals in *Oliver Twist;* **Southwark** was a warren of slums and warehouses; and notorious Seven Dials in **Covent Garden** was the haunt of petty criminals and the dirt poor. Of Dickens's many London homes, only **48 Doughty Street** *(tel 020 7405 2127, ££, dickensmuseum.com),* where he completed *The Pickwick Papers,* wrote *Oliver Twist,* and began *Nicholas Nickleby,* survives.

20th-century Bohemians

The area around the British Museum (see pp. 120–123) also gave its name to one of London's most famous literary circles: the Bloomsbury Group. Novelists Virginia Woolf and E. M. Forster, economist John Maynard Keynes, biographer Lytton Strachey, artist Roger Fry, and poet Clive Bell began meeting at **46 Gordon Square** around 1905, for "the pleasures of human intercourse and the enjoyment of beautiful objects." Their interests were wide-ranging, but they all rebelled against Victorian values, helping to shape modern attitudes to sexuality and equality.

Whereas his cat has a plinth outside his house, Samuel Johnson's statue is in nearby St. Clement Danes.

REVOLUTIONARY **WRITERS**

London has been a haven for revolutionary thinkers. Karl Marx, author of the *Communist Manifesto,* moved here in 1849, living with his family at **28 Dean Street** and working in the British Museum Reading Room. Vladimir Lenin produced his journal—*Iskra*—at 37a Clerkenwell Green, which is now home to the **Marx Memorial Library** *(tel 020 7253 1485, open Mon.–Thurs. 12–4 p.m., marx-memorial-library.org).*

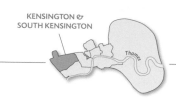

KENSINGTON &
SOUTH KENSINGTON

Kensington & South Kensington

Located to the west of Hyde Park, Kensington (of which South Kensington is a very distinct part) is replete with Gothic-style museum buildings, parks, gardens, and whitewashed Victorian town houses. Part of the Royal Borough of Kensington and Chelsea, the area has royal connections that go back to the 17th century. The future Queen Victoria was born in Kensington Palace in 1819. Her consort, Prince Albert, developed South Kensington into a didactic domain to enlighten Britain's masses in the 19th century. Three world-class museums are here—the Natural History Museum, the Science Museum, and the Victoria and Albert Museum—while the ornate Royal Albert Hall hosts concerts by major international orchestras and performers.

◑ **Kensington Palace's Ceremonial Dress Collection displays historic formal attire worn by members of the royal family.**

KENSINGTON & SOUTH KENSINGTON

Kensington & South Kensington

London's educational heart is filled with glorious Victorian buildings and sumptuous parks.

❼ Kensington Palace (see p. 134) Members of the royal family occupy private apartments in the palace, but the sumptuous state rooms are open to the public. Head west along Kensington High Street to Holland Park.

❽ Holland Park (see p. 135) The Kyoto Garden in Holland Park glows with color in fall. Leave the park by the Ilchester Place exit, and turn onto Holland Park Road.

❾ Leighton House Museum (see p. 135) One of London's finest 19th-century interiors was created by artist Frederic, Lord Leighton.

0 — 800 meters
0 — 800 yards

KENSINGTON & SOUTH KENSINGTON   DISTANCE: 4 MILES (6.5 KM) TIME: APPROX. 8 HOURS TUBE START: SOUTH KENSINGTON

KENSINGTON & SOUTH KENSINGTON

6 Serpentine Gallery (see p. 134)
Each summer an architect-designed
temporary pavilion is erected at the
east end of the gallery. Follow any path
west to reach Kensington Palace.

**5 Royal Albert
Hall & Albert
Memorial** (see
p. 133) The memorial
to Prince Albert, Queen
Victoria's consort, is
close to London's
preeminent concert
hall. Take any path
northeast to reach the
Serpentine Gallery.

KENSINGTON
GARDENS

Serpentine
Gallery

6

The Serpentine

HYDE PARK

Albert
Memorial

5

KNIGHTSBRIDGE

Royal
Albert
Hall

PRINCE
CONSORT
ROAD

EXHIBITION ROAD

QUEEN'S GATE

Brompton
Oratory

BROMPTON ROAD

Science
Museum

4

1

2

3

Victoria and
Albert Museum

Natural
History Museum

BROMPTON RD.

QUEEN'S GATE

OLD BROMPTON RD.

⊖ South
Kensington

4 Science Museum (see pp. 132–133)
Science is made accessible with interactive
displays. Head up Exhibition Road, then
turn west onto Prince Consort Road and
north onto Kensington Gore.

3 Brompton Oratory (see
p. 131) This is London's most opulent
Catholic church. Return to the V&A,
then turn north on Exhibition Road.

1 Natural History Museum
(see pp. 136–137) Start by
exploring the history of living
things, from dinosaurs to Darwin.
Head east on Cromwell Road.

2 Victoria and Albert Museum (see pp. 130–131)
Discover art and design, and admire items such as Tipu
Sultan's tiger. Brompton Oratory is immediately east.

Natural History Museum

1 See pp. 136–137.

Cromwell Rd., SW7 • tel 020 7942 5000 • Closed Dec. 24–26
• Tube: South Kensington • nhm.ac.uk

Victoria and Albert Museum

2 Enter the museum through the extravagantly carved main entrance on Cromwell Road. From architecture and embroidery to fashion spanning the ages and globe, it's all here. On this level, the **Jameel Gallery,** which displays objects from the Islamic Middle East, includes the world's oldest dated carpet—the mid-16th-century **Ardabil Carpet.** Measuring 34 feet by 16 feet (10.5 m by 5 m), and considered one of the finest classical Persian carpets, it adorned a Sufi shrine in the city of Ardabil in northwestern Iran for more than 300 years. Also on this level are the **Raphael Cartoon Court,** which

Monumental sculpture in the Medieval and Renaissance 1350–1600 gallery on Level 1.

displays the Renaissance master's painted designs for tapestries for the Sistine Chapel in Rome, and the **Cast Courts**, a unique assembly of life-size plaster casts of reliefs and sculptures from Roman times to the 19th century. The star is a plaster cast of Michelangelo's masterpiece "**David.**" On Level 1, the **Medieval and Renaissance Galleries 300–1600** includes one of the V&A's five notebooks that belonged to Leonardo da Vinci. Visitors have on-screen access to the notes, which contain some of his most innovative designs. The galleries also hold an exceptional collection of sculpture by the Renaissance master Donatello, including the "**Chellini Madonna**"—a bronze roundel of the Virgin Mary and Child. The **British Galleries 1760–1900,** on Level 3, display historic British decorative objects and furnishings. Entire rooms that were removed from demolished houses are reconstructed. Among them is the **Strawberry Room** (Room 120) in carved, painted pine—a rare example of late 18th-century Gothic Revival style. The underground Sainsbury Gallery, accessed from the sensational new Sackler Courtyard entrance on Exhibition Road, opened in 2017 for temporary avant-garde exhibitions.

Cromwell Rd., SW7 · tel 020 7942 2000 · Closed Dec. 24–26 · Tube: South Kensington · vam.ac.uk

Brompton Oratory

3 Marble pillars, baroque sculptures, and lofty domes make the Brompton Oratory one of London's most richly decorated buildings. Consecrated in 1884, the architect was 29-year-old Englishman Herbert Gribble, but many of the sculptures are baroque, including statues of the Twelve Apostles that were imported from Siena, Italy, and date from the 17th century. The **Lady Altar** is another 17th-century Italian import—originally created for a church in Brescia. Both composer Edward Elgar and movie director Alfred Hitchcock were married in the oratory, and KGB agents used the church as a dead-letter drop during the Cold War.

Brompton Rd., SW7 · tel 020 7808 0900 · Tube: South Kensington · bromptonoratory.co.uk

Science Museum

4 The world of science comes alive with exhibits on five levels, plus a ground-floor IMAX 3D Theatre that screens breathtaking films. Also on the ground floor, the gallery called **Making the Modern World** is dedicated to technological and scientific advances from 1750 to the present day. Here you will find the earliest steam engines, including George Stephenson's 1829 locomotive *Rocket.* Other highlights include Richard Arkwright's spinning machine of 1769, which revolutionized textile production, and the double helix model that biologists Francis Crick and James Watson used to explain the structure of DNA in 1953.

An adjacent room, **Exploring Space** introduces the rockets, space probes, and landers used since *Sputnik 1* shot into space in 1957. A highlight here is an example of the J-2 rocket engine that propelled *Apollo* missions to the moon, along with a model of

A 1935 airplane is one of the exhibits in the Science Museum's Making the Modern World gallery.

the *Eagle* lunar module in which Neil Armstrong and Buzz Aldrin touched down on the moon in 1969. **Legend of Apollo** puts children in control of a flight simulator capsule to perform aerial acrobatics.

Who Am I?, a completely interactive gallery on the first floor, engages visitors with exhibits that help them find out what makes each human being unique—or as they say, "What makes you *you*?" Find out why humans are Earth's most successful species and how memory and relationships shape identity; discover what your voice sounds like; and see how your face changes with age.

Exhibition Rd., SW7 • tel 020 7942 4000 • Closed Dec. 24–26 • Tube: South Kensington • sciencemuseum.org.uk

Royal Albert Hall & Albert Memorial

5 Its layout based on that of ancient Roman amphitheaters, the Royal Albert Hall is a magnificently decorated redbrick building famous for hosting the world's biggest annual series of classical concerts—the BBC Proms. Many rock and pop stars, such as Frank Sinatra, Bob Dylan, and Paul Simon, have also played the Albert Hall, and it was the only venue where the Beatles and the Rolling Stones ever appeared on the same bill. Facing the hall across the road in Kensington Gardens is the 180-foot-tall (55 m) **Albert Memorial,** commemorating Queen Victoria's consort, Prince Albert. An opulent canopy covers the gilded statue of the prince, while surrounding the memorial are ornately carved allegorical figures and a frieze depicting great painters, sculptors, architects, poets, and musicians.

Kensington Gore, SW7 • Tel 020 7589 8212, Box Office: 0845 401 5034 • Tube: South Kensington • royalalberthall.com

GOOD **EATS**

■ BYRON (KENSINGTON)
This is a branch of a small hamburger chain with a reputation for serving London's best Aberdeen-Angus burgers.
222 Kensington High St., W8, tel 020 7361 1717, £££

■ THE KENSINGTON CRÊPERIE
Between South Kensington Tube station and the main museums, this small café serves continental breakfasts, crepes, and waffles.
2–6 Exhibition Rd., SW7, tel 020 7589 8947, £

■ THE V&A CAFÉ
London's best and oldest museum café occupies a beautiful arts-and-crafts room. Self-service counters offer a wide choice of hot food, salads, and sandwiches.
Victoria and Albert Museum, Cromwell Rd., SW7, tel 020 7581 2159, ££

■ WHOLE FOODS MARKET
In this vast emporium, you can buy food for a picnic or choose from 11 bars and four table-service restaurants.
63–97 Kensington High St., W8, tel 020 7368 4500, ££

Serpentine Gallery

6 A former tearoom in Kensington Gardens is now home to one of London's best galleries for contemporary art. The Serpentine Gallery holds temporary exhibitions, and has exhibited work by Gilbert & George, Damien Hirst, Andy Warhol, and Henry Moore, among others. Nearby, the Serpentine Sackler Gallery occupies a former gunpowder store and displays works by emerging and leading artists, designers, and architects commissioned specifically for the gallery. Each summer it commissions a leading international architect to build a temporary pavilion, and the resulting radical and exciting structures by such practitioners as Frank Gehry and Ai Weiwei draw crowds.

Kensington Gardens, W2 • tel 020 7402 6075 • Closed Mon. and between exhibitions • Tube: South Kensington • serpentinegalleries.org

Kensington Palace

7 King William III and Queen Mary II bought the handsome redbrick mansion in 1689, and Sir Christopher Wren redesigned it to royal standards. William suffered from asthma, and the village of Kensington was far from the damp, smoky air by the Thames—and more convenient than the existing palace of Hampton Court in southwest London. A highlight of the palace is the **King's Staircase,** painted with figures from the court of King George I, including Peter—a feral child from the woods of Germany—and the king's Polish page, Ulric. The stairs lead to the **state apartments** and the **royal bedrooms,** where Queen Victoria was born in 1819 and was told of her accession to the throne 18 years later. More recently, Kensington Palace was the marital home of Charles and Diana, Prince and Princess of Wales; after they divorced, Diana stayed here until her death in 1997. The **Sunken Gardens** are based on those at **Hampton Court,** and the grounds have been extensively restored with a terrace café to add to the one in the **Orangery.**

Kensington Gardens, W8 • tel 020 3166 6000 • Closed Dec. 24–26 • £££££ • Tube: High Street Kensington or Queensway • hrp.org.uk

Holland Park

8 This peaceful 55-acre (22 ha) park, reached from the western end of Kensington High Street, is one of London's most romantic green spaces. At its center are the remains of **Holland House,** a large Jacobean mansion built in 1605 and mostly destroyed by World War II bombs, which now houses a youth hostel. Each summer, a huge tent beside Holland House provides the setting for a season of opera. The park is home to strutting peacocks, whose shrill cries reverberate around a series of gardens, including the graceful **Kyoto Garden,** laid out with Japanese plants and features. The café serves snacks all day, and the **Orangery** and the **Ice House** show temporary art exhibitions. For families, the park also offers one of London's best children's adventure playgrounds.

Enter the park on Kensington High St., W8 • Tube: Kensington (Olympia), High Street Kensington, or Holland Park • operahollandpark.com

Leighton House Museum

9 Victorian artist Frederic, Lord Leighton (1830–1896) built this exotic mansion on a quiet Kensington side street. The centerpiece is the **Arab Hall,** covered with some of the thousands of tiles—including Iznik tiles, noted for their dazzling blue—that Leighton brought back from the Ottoman Empire, along with wooden lattice screens from Syria and Egypt. Leighton (the first artist to be made a lord) spent the 30 years he lived here turning the house into a palace of art, filling it with sculptures and some 80 oil paintings of his own, as well as paintings by the Pre-Raphaelites, several of whom were friends.

12 Holland Park Rd., W14 • tel 020 7602 3316 • Closed Tues., Jan. 1–2 and, Dec. 25–28 • ££ • Tube: Kensington (Olympia) or Holland Park • rbkc.gov.uk/museums

A cat peers up at a peacock in one of the mosaics that line Leighton House's exquisite Arab Hall.

Natural History Museum

Cathedral-like galleries make a fitting home for the world's largest, most fascinating natural history collection.

Hintze Hall of the Natural History Museum

From the massive—including numerous dinosaur fossils—to the microscopic, the collections of the Natural History Museum comprise more than 80 million specimens. Here you will find everything from the restored skull of a dodo—among the few surviving remains of the ill-fated bird—to a full-size model of a blue whale to early human fossils. Completed in the 1880s, the building itself is a masterpiece of neo-Romanesque architecture. It is divided into four zones—Green, Blue, Red, and Orange—each with a different focus.

■ GREEN ZONE

This zone, including the Central Hall, presents an overview of the planet's ecology. Highlights include a **Creepy Crawlies gallery,** marine fossils, and bird specimens, from *Archaeopteryx*— the earliest known bird—to modern hummingbirds. On Floor 1, see a copy of the tiny skeleton of five-million-year-old **"Lucy,"** one of the first humanlike creatures to walk upright.

■ BLUE ZONE

This ground-floor area to the left of the Central Hall has a major dinosaur gallery dominated by *Diplodocus* and *Triceratops* **skeletons** and an animatronic model of a *Tyrannosaurus rex*. In the mammals gallery you can inspect a suspended model of a blue whale—larger than any dinosaur.

■ RED ZONE

Reached via a side entrance on Exhibition Road, this zone focuses on the forces that shape the Earth. On view are one of the planet's oldest rocks (dating back around 3.85 billion years), fluorescent minerals, and a piece of moon rock brought back

SAVVY **TRAVELER**

In a tucked-away corner of the museum's Green Zone, the **Vault** displays a sparkling array of gemstones, metals, and meteorites. The stars of the collection include naturally colored diamonds and the Nakhla meteorite, which fell from Mars to Earth in 1911.

by the Apollo 16 mission. On the mezzanine is an interactive **Earth Lab,** with staff on hand to answer questions. On Floor 2, watch footage of volcanic eruptions and step inside a simulator mimicking the effects of the 1995 Kobe earthquake on a supermarket.

■ ORANGE ZONE

Enter this zone via the Blue Zone. Its state-of-the-art **Darwin Centre** is built in the shape of a cocoon. Take the elevator to Floor 7, then descend a walkway that allows you to view hundreds of plant and insect specimens. You can also take part in interactive activities and see scientists at work. Back on the ground floor, visit the **Attenborough Studio** to watch films, talk with staff, and handle live specimens, such as a python or tarantula.

Cromwell Rd., SW7 • tel 020 7942 5000 • Closed Dec. 24–26 • Donation expected • Tube: South Kensington • nhm.ac.uk

KENSINGTON & SOUTH KENSINGTON

Parks & Gardens

The Royal Parks owe their existence to the stubborn resolve of successive monarchs to hunt game even when residing in their urban palaces. Large, rural retreats were supplemented in the 19th century by newly created urban parks and legally protected areas of undeveloped wasteland (heath) and woodland. The population density of London is half that of Paris or New York thanks to the generous supply of green spaces.

Equestrians use Rotten Row (above) in Hyde Park. In St. James's Park (right), the view east along the lake offers a glimpse of William Kent's Horse Guards building.

Royal Parks

In medieval times, when London was confined within city walls, much of what is now the metropolis was forest. Hunting was a popular pursuit and one that kings were loath to abandon as the city grew. In 1532, King Henry VIII confiscated the area now occupied by **St. James's Park** from Westminster Abbey and stocked it with deer and other game for his own amusement. Four years later, the king took over the manor of Hyde and added it to his hunting ground to form what is now **Hyde Park.** Farther out, **Richmond Park** and **Greenwich Park** were enclosed in the 15th and 17th centuries respectively.

King Charles I was the first monarch to open the Royal Parks to the public, admitting his subjects to Hyde Park in 1637. In 1730, Queen Caroline, wife of King George II, initiated the creation of the sinuous **Serpentine lake** at the heart of Hyde Park. She also directed the laying out of **Kensington Gardens** on the western side of the Serpentine. In 1872, an act of Parliament designated the northeast tip of Hyde Park as a place where people could stand

KENSINGTON & SOUTH KENSINGTON

up and express their views, however subversive, and the spot became known as **Speaker's Corner.** In the southwest of the park, the **Diana, Princess of Wales Memorial Fountain,** designed by American Kathryn Gustafson, is a popular destination.

Parks for the People

Municipal parks were first created in the Victorian era in response to overcrowded conditions in the rapidly expanding city. The first to open was **Victoria Park** in the East End in 1841. Elsewhere wide stretches of heath and woods were saved from the builders as the city grew. Most famous of these is **Hampstead Heath,** which, with its mix of sporting activities, walking trails, quiet corners, and cultural events typifies London's open spaces.

PARK PERFORMANCES

Holland Park Holds an open-air opera season each summer. **Kensington High Street or Holland Park, W8, operahollandpark.com**

Hyde Park Music events, including Proms in the Park, feature world-famous acts. **Hyde Park, W2, royalparks .org.uk**

Regents Park The open-air theater stages plays through the summer. **Regents Park, NW1, royalparks.org.uk**

Victoria Park Has music on summer weekends and Lovebox Festival in July. **Hackney, E9, towerhamlets.gov.uk**

KENSINGTON & SOUTH KENSINGTON

Afternoon Tea

Served between 3 and 5 p.m., afternoon tea can be a luxurious event, involving delicate china and fanned napkins as well as the culinary essentials of exquisite teas, dainty cakes, and elegant sandwiches. It is a quintessentially English tradition for which London is famous, perfect before a trip to the theater.

■ HIGH CLASS TEAS

To take tea in a royal home, visit Kensington Palace's 18th-century **Pavilion** (*Kensington Palace, W8, tel 020 3166 6113, ££*), where you choose from more than ten flavors of tea, served with homemade cakes and sandwiches.

The official tea sommelier at **The Lanesborough** (*Hyde Park Corner, SW1, tel 020 7333 7250, £££££*) will help you select among exotic options like Dragon Well green tea or Wild Tuo Cha, aged for 17 years to concentrate its flavor. **The Goring** (*Beeston Pl., SW1, tel 020 7396 9000, £££££*) in Victoria offers traditional English teatime fare, notably freshly baked scones with Devonshire clotted cream and jam.

Both the **Ritz** (*150 Piccadilly, W1, 020 7300 2345, £££££*) and, in Mayfair, **Brown's Hotel** (*Albemarle St., W15, tel 020 7493 6020, ££££*) serve dainty sandwiches, scones, and cakes from three-tiered cake stands—with Champagne if you are feeling extravagant. At Brown's, you can schedule a tea-torial to learn sugary secrets from the house pastry chef. Also in Mayfair, the **Connaught's** (*Carlos Pl., W1, tel 020 7107 8861, £££££*) "Chic and Shock" afternoon tea adds just a few haute gourmet twists to the tradition, such as raspberry and violet jam, and smoked-salmon-with-wasabi-cream finger sandwiches.

■ MUSEUM TEA ROOMS

Tea at the **National Gallery** (*Trafalgar Sq., WC2, 020 7747 2525, ££*) is an utterly British experience, with local ingredients and homemade preserves. Next door you can have tea on the top floor of the **National Portrait Gallery** (*St. Martin's Pl., WC2, tel 020 7312 2490, £££*) with panoramic views over London. The **Wallace Collection** (*Manchester Sq., W1, tel 020 7563 9505, ££*), in Marylebone, displays some

KENSINGTON & SOUTH KENSINGTON

Scones, jam tarts, and a cream-filled sponge cake are regular components of afternoon tea.

of the best French paintings, porcelain, and furniture anywhere outside of France. The afternoon tea is also distinctly French, featuring foie gras, salmon tartare, and French pastries.

■ TRENDY TEAS

Londoners book weeks in advance to experience Piccadilly's **Sketch** (*9 Conduit St., W1, tel 020 7659 4500, £££*), a concept space dedicated to both art and food. But no reservations are taken at the more casual Parlour gallery, which serves afternoon tea. Enjoy colorful macaroons while keeping an eye open for lounging fashionistas.

For something even less traditional and equally fashionable, try afternoon "Cocktails and Cupcakes" at Mayfair's **The May Fair** (*Stratton St., W1, tel 020 7915 3892, £££*). It may not be tea for the family, but it is hard to pass up the bar's tea-inspired cocktails and cupcakes.

■ GREAT VALUE TEAS

With its floral wallpaper, **Bea's of Bloomsbury** (*44 Theobalds Rd., WC1, tel 020 7278 7949, ££££*) is a baking paradise devoted to colorful cupcakes and dense brownies. They also serve a wonderful afternoon tea, at a fraction of the cost of the big hotels.

CHELSEA POTTER

CHELSEA POTTER

CHELSEA,
BELGRAVIA, &
KNIGHTSBRIDGE

Chelsea, Belgravia, & Knightsbridge

These three neighborhoods are home to some of London's wealthiest people. The streets abound with chic boutiques and opulent department stores, including Harrods, London's most exclusive emporium. This luxurious consumption is juxtaposed with elegant churches, a hospital for military veterans, and a 17th-century garden dedicated to the healing powers of plants. In Victorian times, Chelsea was an artists' quarter, and the works of many of its residents—including Whistler, Rossetti, and Turner—can be seen in Tate Britain. Today, it is the Saatchi Gallery that sets the artistic pace with its exhibitions of contemporary art. Literary figures lived here, too: Visit the home of social critic Thomas Carlyle, known as the "sage of Chelsea."

◀ **Swinging Sixties music idols such as Jimi Hendrix and the Rolling Stones were aficionados of the Chelsea Potter pub on King's Road.**

Chelsea, Belgravia, & Knightsbridge

Combine high-end shopping in Knightsbridge with visits to galleries and churches, and enjoy a quiet interlude in the Chelsea Physic Garden.

1 Harrods (see pp. 146–147) **Start at London's flagship store, where luxury pervades. On leaving, walk east on Brompton Road and Knightsbridge, then turn right onto Wilton Place.**

9 Carlyle's House (see p. 151) **Visit the home of the Victorian writer Thomas Carlyle, one of the many former local residents who gave Chelsea its literary and artistic character.**

8 Chelsea Old Church (see p. 151) A statue of St. Thomas More, erected in 1969, stands outside the church near his home. Return east on Cheyne Walk and turn left onto Cheyne Row.

St. Paul's Church, Knightsbridge

Hyde Park Corner

KNIGHTSBRIDGE

Knightsbridge

BELGRAVE SQUARE

Harrods

BROMPTON ROAD
BEAUCHAMP PL
PONT STREET
SLOANE STREET

BROMPTON RD

South Kensington

Gloucester Road

Sloane Square

OLD BROMPTON ROAD
ONSLOW SQ.

SLOANE AVENUE

The Saatchi Gallery

King's Road

CHELTENHAM TERRACE

CHELSEA

FULHAM ROAD
SYDNEY STREET

SOUTH KENSINGTON

KING'S ROAD

Royal Hospital Chelsea

RANELAGH GARDENS

OLD CHURCH

CHELSEA

FLOOD STREET

ROYAL HOSPITAL RD.

CHELSEA EMBANKMENT

Carlyle's House

OAKLEY STREET

Chelsea Physic Garden

Chelsea Old Church

ALBERT BRIDGE

| 0 | | 800 meters |
| 0 | | 800 yards |

CHELSEA, BELGRAVIA, & KNIGHTSBRIDGE   DISTANCE: 6 MILES (9.6 KM) TIME: APPROX. 8.5 HOURS   TUBE START: KNIGHTSBRIDGE

❷ St. Paul's Church, Knightsbridge (see p. 147) The Victorian church's plain facade belies a rich interior. Take the tube from Hyde Park Corner to Pimlico.

❸ Tate Britain (see pp. 152–153) View the best of British art from the 16th century until today. Take the Tube from Pimlico to Sloane Square.

❹ The Saatchi Gallery (see p. 148) Expect a few surprises at reclusive advertising guru Charles Saatchi's contemporary art gallery, then stroll west on King's Road.

❺ King's Road (see p. 148) Running southwest from Sloane Square, Chelsea's main thoroughfare never goes out of fashion. Turn south onto Cheltenham Terrace toward Royal Hospital Road.

❼ Chelsea Physic Garden (see p. 150) Founded by the ancient Company of Apothecaries, the garden is a showcase for healing plants. On leaving, turn left on Royal Hospital Road and continue west on Chelsea Embankment to Old Church Street.

❻ Royal Hospital Chelsea (see p. 149) Visit the home of scarlet-coated Chelsea Pensioners, which is also the site of the annual Chelsea Flower Show, then continue west on Royal Hospital Road.

Harrods

1 Emblazoned with the motto "All Things for All People Everywhere," Harrods has been supplying luxury goods and services to a wealthy worldwide clientele for almost two centuries. From a one-room grocery shop founded by Charles Henry Harrod in 1849, the business has expanded into high-end fashion, perfumes, luxury food, electronics, jewelry, furniture, stationery, gifts, kitchen appliances, sports equipment (including golf carts), and even rabbits, gerbils, and puppies. You can have a suit made to order or engage a personal shopper. Doormen attired in trademark olive-green livery usher customers across the threshold but turn away anyone not considered appropriately dressed. Inside, glittering displays vie for attention in hundreds of departments on seven floors. The highlight is the **Food Hall**—a confection of tilework and mosaic friezes by 19th-century sculptor W. J. Neatby—where

Harrods' Food Hall tempts shoppers with an assortment of fish, oysters, and caviar.

artistically displayed meat and fish, patisseries, fruit, and vegetables tingle the tastebuds. Aside from the Food Hall, there are more than **30 other eateries,** from the ground-floor Parisian tearoom to the fifth-floor Georgian restaurant. Another must-see sight is the **Egyptian Hall,** festooned with statues and art mimicking ancient Egypt, where former Harrods owner Mohammed Al-Fayed built a shrine to his son Dodi and Princess Diana, who died together in 1997.

87–135 Brompton Rd., SW1 • tel 020 7730 1234 • Closed Easter Sun. and Dec. 25—27 • Tube: Knightsbridge • harrods.com

St. Paul's Church, Knightsbridge

2 The parish church of Knightsbridge is celebrated as much for its parishioners as for its high Victorian style. The 1st Duke of Wellington (1769–1852), vanquisher of Napoleon, who lived on nearby Hyde Park Corner, was a regular worshiper in the church's early days. Today's celebrities may be seen at the Christmas carol service. St. Paul's was built in 1843 with a fashionably plain facade that belies a richly decorated interior. Elegant cast-iron pillars support galleries on three sides. George Frederick Bodley, a specialist in the Gothic Revival style, designed the reredos behind the altar and the carved rood screen separating the nave from the chancel, both of which were added in 1892. On the walls of the nave, tiled panels by Daniel Bell (1870s) depicting the life of Christ are interspersed with scenes from the crucifixion by Gerald Moira (1920s). Throughout, paintings and statues of people connected with the history of St. Paul's are on view.

32a Wilton Pl., SW1 • tel 020 7201 9999 • Tube: Knightsbridge or Hyde Park Corner • stpaulsknightsbridge.org

GOOD EATS

■ **RABBIT**
Modern British food with flair highlights the menu at this faux-farm restaurant serving English wines, plus sharing plates that include rabbit ravioli. **172 Kings Rd., SW3, tel 020 3750 0172, £££**

■ **THE GRENADIER**
Once the Grenadier Guards' officers' mess, the mews pub brims with military souvenirs. Snack on sandwiches in the bar or eat in the restaurant. **18 Wilton Row, SW1, tel 020 7235 3074, £££**

■ **HARVEY NICHOLS**
Start the day with a full English breakfast or freshly squeezed juice and pastries at the Fifth Floor Café and Terrace. Lunch, tea, and dinner are also served. **109–125 Knightsbridge, SW1, tel 020 7235 5250, ££££** (see p. 156)

Tate Britain

3 See pp. 152–153.

Millbank, SW1 • tel 020 7887 8888 • Closed Dec. 24–26 • Visitors wishing to see particular works should call in advance • Tube: Pimlico • tate.org.uk

The Saatchi Gallery

4 They may be thought-provoking, controversial, even outrageous, but the exhibitions at one of Britain's leading galleries for contemporary art are never uninteresting. Founded by art collector and advertising magnate Charles Saatchi, the current gallery occupies a former army headquarters, whose airy white rooms give the artworks and installations space to shine. The gallery has exhibited pioneering 20th-century artists such as Jeff Koons, Tracey Emin, and Damien Hirst, and new talent is often showcased. Provocative art has given way in recent years to more mainstream exhibitions including, in 2019, of Tutankhamun's treasures. And since 2018 the gallery has hosted the FairForSaatchi art fair, in June.

King's Rd., SW3 • tel 020 7811 3070 • Tube: Sloane Square • saatchigallery.com

IN **THE KNOW**

In 1764, eight-year-old Wolfgang Amadeus Mozart composed his first symphony while staying at **180 Ebury Street**, just a few streets south of King's Road. The building is marked with a plaque.

King's Road

5 The Swinging Sixties brought boutiques and psychedelia to the King's Road. Since then, gentrification has changed the style, but the street has retained its reputation for stylish shopping. In Sloane Square the **Royal Court Theatre** (*Sloane Sq., tel 020 7565 5000, royalcourttheatre.com*) challenges audiences with its avant-garde productions, while clothing boutiques such as punk fashion designer Vivienne Westwood's **World's End** (*430 King's Rd., tel 020 7352 6551, worldsendshop.co.uk*) and interior design stores are interspersed with pubs and restaurants along the King's Road itself.

King's Rd., between Sloane Sq. and Waterford Rd. • Tube: Sloane Square • kingsroad.chelsea.london

Formal dress for Chelsea Pensioners is based on an 18th-century British Army uniform.

Royal Hospital Chelsea

6 This 17th-century redbrick building designed by Sir Christopher Wren "for the succor and relief of veterans broken by age and war" is still home to British Army veterans known as Chelsea Pensioners. A golden statue by Grinling Gibbons of King Charles II forms the centerpiece of the **Figure Court.** The **Chapel** and the large porticoed entrance to the **Great Hall** where the pensioners dine dominate one side of the court and the Long Wards, where they sleep in wainscoted berths, forms the other two sides. You can see a mock-up of their berths in the hospital's small **museum.** In spring, the grounds are transformed into gardens for the annual Chelsea Flower Show.

Royal Hospital Rd., SW3 • tel 020 7881 5200 • Closed Sat., Sun., bank holidays, and for hospital events • Groups of up to 10 people can visit (but not view the museum and Long Wards) 10 a.m.–12 a.m. and 1:30 p.m.–3:30 p.m. • Tours (£££, including museum and Long Wards) 10 a.m. and 1:30 p.m. • Tube: Sloane Square • chelsea-pensioners.org.uk

Chelsea Physic Garden

7 Sheltered behind high walls, this 4-acre (1.6 ha) garden was founded for medicinal research and education by the Society of Apothecaries in 1673. Many of the plants nurtured here have contributed to the development of commonly used drugs, such as aspirin, which was derived from the meadowsweet herb. Plants like this can be seen in the **Pharmaceutical Garden,** while the **Garden of World Medicine** features healing plants favored by tribal communities. Flowers used in perfumes and aromatherapy are on show throughout the garden. The shop sells plants and, from August to September, honey from its bees.

66 Royal Hospital Rd., SW3 • tel 020 7352 5646 • Closed Sat., April–Oct., Sat.–Sun. Nov.–March • ££-£££ • Tube: Sloane Square • chelseaphysicgarden.co.uk

Sir Hans Sloane provided the land for the Chelsea Physic Garden, and his statue keeps watch there.

Chelsea Old Church

8 Although the restored redbrick exterior creates the impression that this is a modern church, the building actually dates from the 13th century and is reportedly the place where King Henry VIII married his third wife, Jane Seymour, in 1536. The church includes a chapel that was rebuilt by Henry's onetime advisor and lord chancellor, Sir Thomas More, who lived close by. **More's Chapel** was one of the few parts of the church to survive bomb damage in World War II. A group of rare books, including a Bible from 1717, a 1723 prayer book, and a Homilies from 1683, also survived and are the only **chained books** in a London church—the practice of chaining books to shelves or reading desks was a way of preventing theft in a time when books were rare and valuable.

2 Old Church St., SW3 • tel 020 7795 1019 • Tube: South Kensington or Sloane Square • chelseaoldchurch.org.uk

Carlyle's House

9 The Scottish writer and historian Thomas Carlyle was one of Victorian London's foremost men of letters. He was known as "the sage of Chelsea," and many notable guests, including author Charles Dickens, novelist George Eliot, philosopher John Stuart Mill, poet Alfred Lord Tennyson, and naturalist Charles Darwin, visited. Carlyle also wrote many of his best known books here, including *The French Revolution,* which he had to write a second time since the first copy was accidentally burnt by Mill's maid. In 1895, only 14 years after his death, Carlyle's home was opened to the public and has been kept how it was when he lived here. The building dates from the early 18th century and sits on one of London's best preserved Georgian streets. Inside are paintings by American artist James McNeill Whistler, as well as books, furniture, and personal effects belonging to Carlyle and his wife, Jane—herself a prominent essayist. A highlight is Carlyle's much loved garden, including a fig tree that still produces fruit.

SAVVY **TRAVELER**

For antiques and art, head to **Pimlico Road,** just south of Sloane Square, which has a large choice of specialty shops selling everything from 17th-century paintings to fine contemporary furniture.

24 Cheyne Row, SW3 • tel 020 7352 7087 • ££ • Closed Mon., Tues., and Nov.–Feb. • Tube: Sloane Square or South Kensington • nationaltrust.org.uk

Tate Britain

The original Tate gallery is dedicated to the work of British artists and artists resident in Britain.

Tate Britain has the world's largest collection of J. M. W. Turner's work, including "The Blue Rigi."

Founded in 1897 on the art collection of sugar baron Sir Henry Tate, Tate Britain

is the world center for the study of British art. The main exhibit, a 500-year

"Walk Through British Art" features 500 works of art, displayed chronologically

in two sections divided by a central exhibition hall. There are also eight

Spotlight Displays focusing on a particular period or theme, which change twice

a year. In the fall, the gallery displays work by artists shortlisted for the Turner

Prize, a prestigious award presented to a British artist under the age of 50.

■ THE BRITISH TRADITION

The main exhibit starts in the western galleries with Hans Holbein, court painter to Henry VIII, and proceeds to other leading lights in British art. Among the works on display are John Constable's **"Flatford Mill"** (1816–1817) and John William Waterhouse's **"The Lady of Shallot"** (1888).

Popular draws are works by the Pre-Raphaelites, including Dante Gabriel Rossetti and John Everett Millais, who used bright colors and recalled a lost romantic world. Millais' **"Ophelia,"** depicting the drowning Shakespearean heroine, is a perennial favorite.

■ THE MODERNS

The east galleries begin in 1930 and include Francis Bacon's **"Three Studies for Figures at the Base of a Crucifixion"** from 1944 and Lucian Freud's **"Girl With a Kitten."** In 1939, **"Recumbant Figure"** became the first of many sculptures by Henry Moore to be acquired by the Tate, and Moore is one of a number of artists to have a large gallery all to himself. The walk continues, via David Hockney (**"A Bigger Splash"**), to the Young British Artists of the 1980s. **"Forms without**

Life" is a wall-mounted display cabinet of seashells by Damien Hirst, winner of the 1995 Turner Prize.

■ THE DUVEEN GALLERIES

The vast, pillared halls in the center of the Tate hold temporary exhibitions and special installations. In spring and fall, the space provides a dramatic catwalk during London Fashion Week.

■ MASTER OF LIGHT & ATMOSPHERE

J. M. W. Turner's watercolors, drawings, and oils fill the **Clore Wing**. Check out his late paintings, especially **"Sunrise with Sea Monsters"** (circa 1845), in which forms dissolve in shimmering light. Two upper rooms display changing works by the mystic and poet William Blake, including **"Tyger"** and other original illustrations from his collection of poems *Songs of Innocence and Experience.*

CHELSEA, BELGRAVIA, & KNIGHTSBRIDGE

Millbank, SW1 • tel 020 7887 8888 • Closed Dec. 24–26 • Visitors wishing to see a particular work should call in advance to check if it is on display • Tube: Pimlico • tate.org.uk

Caught on Canvas

Portrait painters, landscape artists, French Impressionists—all have been inspired by London and its people over the centuries, creating a vast archive of the city's changing face. Van Dyck painted King Charles I, Canaletto captured the city's pageantry and architecture, Whistler the waterside, and Turner the Houses of Parliament. Today, London shines at the cutting edge of contemporary art.

Hogarth & Turner

Two of London's best known artists are William Hogarth and J. M. W Turner. Hogarth was a satirist who often portrayed the less salubrious side of the city, for example "A Rake's Progress" (circa 1735), which depicts gambling dens and brothels in a sobering story of fecklessness and corruption.

In the 19th century, romantic landscape artist Turner was fascinated by weather and light effects, which can be seen in his numerous impressionistic watercolor studies of the dramatic burning of the Houses of Parliament in 1834.

Artists from Abroad

Many foreign artists have been drawn to London, often for royal patronage. In the 16th century, German portrait painter Hans Holbein found favor with King Henry VIII, and a century later, baroque artists Peter Paul Rubens and Anthony van Dyck were both knighted by King Charles I.

The cityscape has also inspired. Venetian artist Canaletto painted the River Thames 48 times in the 1750s, and American James McNeill Whistler was also taken with the river when he moved to London in 1859. So was Claude Monet, who painted the smoggy Thames at Westminster during a stay in London in 1870–1871. The view lured him back again in 1899–1901, resulting in his "Houses of Parliament" series.

Contemporary Viewpoint

In the early 1990s, the city's art scene began making its presence felt in East London's Spitalfields, Shoreditch, and Hoxton. The duo Gilbert & George predate the arrival of younger artists in the area, having lived close to Brick Lane for more than 30 years. Their "Twenty London East One Pictures" of 2004–2005 ranged rows of street names of their own E1 postcode around images of their gesticulating selves—an unexpected piece for a cluster of streets that were once no-go areas.

ARTIST'S **HOMES**

John Constable (1776–1837) 40 Well Walk, NW3

Vincent van Gogh (1853–1890) 87 Hackford Road, SW9

Dante Gabriel Rossetti (1828–1882) 110 Hallam Street, W1

J. M. W. Turner (1775–1851) 40 Sandycoombe Road, TW1

James McNeill Whistler (1834–1903) 96 Cheyne Walk, SW10

Whistler would often paint scenes from memory in his Chelsea studio (above). The mist in this (left) and Monet's other London paintings was actually smog, which blighted the city at that time.

CHELSEA, BELGRAVIA, & KNIGHTSBRIDGE

Designer Knightsbridge

Dazzling boutiques and designer shops located near the upscale Harrods and Harvey Nichols stores provide some serious shopping opportunities for Knightsbridge's wealthy residents. Local British designers, classic Italian names, and specialists for accessories and shoes are all represented.

■ HARRODS

London's flagship store (see pp. 146–147) stocks a wide selection of designer labels, including Balmain, Victoria Beckham, Chloé, Dior, Stella McCartney, Alexander McQueen, Paul Smith, and Valentino.

■ HARVEY NICHOLS

Many local people choose not to face the crowds at Harrods and instead enjoy shopping at "Harvey Nicks," a chic alternative with eight floors of designer collections and a huge beauty department. The store originally opened as a linen shop in 1813 and still includes an impressive range of home products. The top level features a restaurant, bar, café, and food market.

109–125 Knightsbridge, SW1 • tel 020 7235 5000 • Closed Easter Sun. and Dec. 25 • Tube: Knightsbridge • harveynichols.com

■ SLOANE STREET BOUTIQUES

If the big department stores are overwhelming, Sloane Street is lined by small boutiques dedicated to famous designers such as **Giorgio Armani** (*37–42 Sloane St., SW1*). Other designer stores along here are **Gucci** (*18 Sloane St., SW1*), **Prada** (*43–45 Sloane St., SW1*), **Dior** (*31 Sloane St., SW1*), **Paule Ka** (*167–169 Sloane St., SW1*), **Chanel** (*135 Sloane St., SW1*), **Saint Laurent** (*171–172 Sloane St., SW1*), and **Alberta Ferretti** (*205–206 Sloane St., SW1*), to name a few. These smaller shops often have exclusive products from the latest collections. There are also some exquisite lingerie shops here, such as **La Perla** (*163 Sloane St., SW1*), which specializes in elegant Italian designs, and around the corner, **Rigby & Peller** (*2 Hans Road, SW3*), which supplies underwear to the royal family.

CHELSEA, BELGRAVIA, & KNIGHTSBRIDGE

Sloane Street has become London's top shopping district, with designer stores such as Prada.

■ BRITISH DESIGNS

If you're looking for top British brands, head to **Jo Malone** (*150 Sloane St., SW1*) for luxury fragrances for the home, bath, and body; **Anya Hindmarsh** (*157–158 Sloane St., SW1*) for superb craftsmanship in fine leather and cashmere, with a touch of humor; and **Pickett** (*149 Sloane St., SW1*) for stylish handbags, luggage, and personalized folios. **Caroline Charles** (*56–57 Beauchamp Pl., SW1*) has been designing colorful and highly wearable clothes for women since the 1960s and is a favorite among stylish royals and celebrities.

■ SHOES

Strap on your Jimmy Choos or stomp along in your Church's Oxfords to find a few extra pairs of shoes. Check out the ageless **Crockett & Jones** (*155 Brompton Rd., SW1*), beloved by grandfathers and hipsters alike, while **Russell & Bromley** (*77 Brompton Rd., SW1*) provides classic, stylish shoes for men and women. Or choose from the amazing Italians, **Botega Veneta** (*33 Sloane St., SW1*), or **Salvatore Ferragamo** (*207 Sloane St., SW1*). And, of course, pick up a pair of one-of-a-kind heels from **Jimmy Choo** (*32 Sloane St., SW1*).

East London

Traditionally home of dockworkers and immigrants, East London is Britain's capital at its multicultural best and holds some of its most vibrant attractions. The Tower of London has been England's most important fortress (and prison) for almost a thousand years and is still charged with protecting the Crown Jewels. Close by is Tower Bridge, where you can take its high-level walk across the Thames for panoramic river views. If you're lucky, you may see the bridge open below for a ship to pass through. A Tube stop north brings you to the Whitechapel, one of London's leading contemporary art galleries. Nearby are Shoreditch and Spitalfields, known for their exciting street fashion and art galleries. Farther east is Queen Elizabeth Olympic Park, site of the 2012 Games. At Canary Wharf, where the river loops south, gleaming office towers rise above the revitalized Docklands area. Opposite, at Greenwich on the south bank of the Thames, the tea clipper *Cutty Sark,* the Old Royal Naval College, and the National Maritime Museum evoke London's maritime past.

❶ **The Yeoman Warders and the colony of ravens are popular attractions at the Tower of London.**

East London

Discover history, elegance, and culture in a Thames-side setting.

EAST LONDON

❹ Queen Elizabeth Olympic Park (see pp. 163–164) The site of the 2012 Olympic Games is now a leisure park, with great shopping opportunities in London's largest mall. Take the Docklands Light Railway (DLR) to Canary Wharf.

❸ Whitechapel Gallery (see p. 163) In the heart of the East End, the gallery has temporary exhibitions of modern art. Return to Aldgate East. Take a Tube to Stratford International, changing at Mile End.

❷ Tower Bridge (see pp. 162–163) Explore the bridge and take in the views from the upper walkways. Take the Tube from Tower Hill to Aldgate East.

❶ Tower of London (see pp. 168–169) The original keep was constructed by William the Conqueror. Walk around to Tower Bridge Approach.

**EAST LONDON   DISTANCE: 11 MILES (17.5 KM)
TIME: APPROX. 9 HOURS   TUBE START: TOWER HILL**

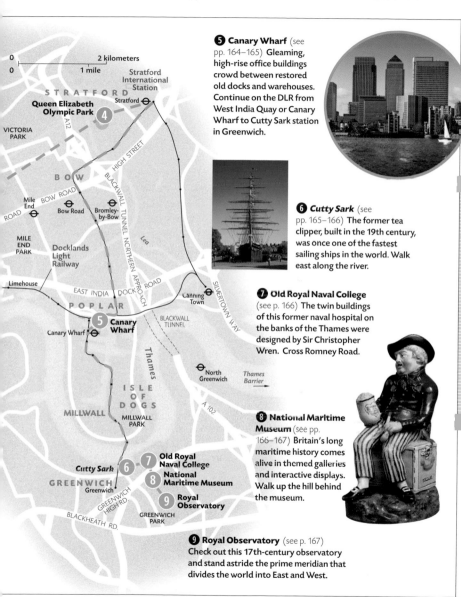

❺ Canary Wharf (see pp. 164–165) Gleaming, high-rise office buildings crowd between restored old docks and warehouses. Continue on the DLR from West India Quay or Canary Wharf to Cutty Sark station in Greenwich.

❻ Cutty Sark (see pp. 165–166) The former tea clipper, built in the 19th century, was once one of the fastest sailing ships in the world. Walk east along the river.

❼ Old Royal Naval College (see p. 166) The twin buildings of this former naval hospital on the banks of the Thames were designed by Sir Christopher Wren. Cross Romney Road.

❽ National Maritime Museum (see pp. 166–167) Britain's long maritime history comes alive in themed galleries and interactive displays. Walk up the hill behind the museum.

❾ Royal Observatory (see p. 167) Check out this 17th-century observatory and stand astride the prime meridian that divides the world into East and West.

EAST LONDON

EAST LONDON

Tower of London

1 See pp. 168–169.

Tower of London, Tower Hill, EC3 • tel 020 3166 6000 • Closed Jan. 1 and Dec. 24–26 • £££££ • Tube: Tower Hill • hrp.org.uk/toweroflondon

Tower Bridge

2 Built in 1894, London's most famous bridge solved the problem of how to build a bridge for the city's East End that would also allow ships to enter the busiest port in the world. The answer lay in the bridge's lower span; its two halves can be raised, drawbridge-style, to let ships pass through. The pinnacled towers, which conceal the lifting mechanism, now house the **Tower Bridge Exhibition.** The high-level walkways between them provide breathtaking views of the river and some of London's best-known sites, including St. Paul's Cathedral and the London Eye to the west and Canary Wharf and Greenwich to the east. Glass floors give a bird's-eye view directly below. The bridge-opening system was electrified in 1974, but in

Despite having two towers of its own, Tower Bridge is named for the Tower of London.

the **Victorian engine room** below the South Tower, you can see the massive steam-powered pumps that drove the original lifting mechanism. In its early years, the bridge was raised more than 20 times a day. Now it is raised up to three times a day to let through tall-masted sailing ships, naval vessels, and cruise ships.

Tower Bridge Rd., SE1 • tel 020 7403 3761 • Closed Dec. 24–26 • £££ • Tube: Tower Hill • towerbridge.org.uk

Whitechapel Gallery

3 Founded on the principle that art can inspire and lift the spirit, the Whitechapel opened in 1901. Since then, its program of temporary exhibitions has brought some of contemporary art's biggest names—including Pablo Picasso, Jackson Pollock, Frida Kahlo, and Lucien Freud, among others—to this traditionally deprived area of London. The gallery also has a movie theater, a good art bookshop, a lively café, and an elegant restaurant.

77–82 Whitechapel High St., E1 • tel 020 7522 7888 • Closed Mon. • Some temporary exhibitions £££ • Tube: Aldgate East • whitechapelgallery.org

SAVVY **TRAVELER**

The **Emirates Aviation Experience** (*Edmund Halley Way, SE10, tel 020 3440 7020, aviation-experience.com*) teaches about aviation and has four state-of-the-art flight simulators. Then, soar 295 feet (90 m) above the Thames and O2 Arena event stadium on the Emirates Air Link cable-car (*emiratesairline. gttix.com*).

Queen Elizabeth Olympic Park

4 The 2012 Olympics left London with a legacy of a park, a mall, and some cleaned-up waterways, developed mainly from a disused industrial area. **Westfield Stratford City** was built as the entrance to the Games, and the mall, said to be the largest in a European city, with more than 350 stores, has become a popular destination. The park, which has 22 miles (35 km) of cycle trails and footpaths, and 4 miles (6 km) of waterways, has been landscaped around the River Lea, which flows through here to the Thames. The main **Olympic Stadium** has been reduced in height for use by local soccer team, West Ham, and will continue to be used for athletics. The Olympic aquatic

EAST LONDON

Anish Kapoor's sculpture dominates the skyline at the Queen Elizabeth Olympic Park.

center, designed by Zaha Hadid to international acclaim, has two 50-meter pools. Now called the **London Aquatics Centre,** it is open to the public daily. The park stages open-air music events, and on weekends 45-minute boat trips set off from the quay. For a panorama of the park, visitors can climb the **ArcelorMittal Orbit,** Britain's largest sculpture, designed by Anish Kapoor and featuring the world's longest tunnel slide and the UK's tallest free-fall rappel. In 2019, a massive expansion was launched that will add major cultural venues, from Sadler's Wells to the Smithsonian Institute.

Stratford, E20 • ArcelorMittal Orbit ££££ • Tube: Stratford • queenelizabetholympicpark.co.uk

Canary Wharf

5 On the Isle of Dogs—a former island bounded on three sides by a huge loop in the river—a group of gleaming skyscrapers rise from London's former docklands. The development, known as Canary Wharf, stands on the site of the 18th-century docks of the old West India Company, which supplied Britain with rum, sugar, chocolate, and other treats from the New World. The skycrapers house the world headquarters of many leading financial and media companies, while well-preserved warehouses brim with bars and restaurants, and office workers relax near small-craft moorings. The **Museum of London Docklands,** housed in an old sugar warehouse (No. 1 Warehouse) on West India Quay, recounts London's history as a trading city from Roman times through to the 21st century. Three floors are packed with models, art, and documents illustrating the life and times of the communities that lived and worked along the river, and the busy backstreets have been imaginatively reconstructed. In the Mudlarks children's gallery, kids can weigh cargo or load a tea clipper.

Canary Wharf, E14 • Museum of London Docklands: West India Quay, E14; tel 020 7001 9844; closed Dec. 24–26 • Tube: Canary Wharf; DLR: Canary Wharf • museumoflondon .org.uk/docklands

Cutty Sark

6
You can spot the tip of the 152-foot (46.3 m) mast of this seafaring treasure above the surrounding buildings as you approach the dry dock where it rests on the south bank of the Thames. Launched in 1869, the *Cutty Sark* was one of the world's fastest ships. It began as a tea clipper, taking part in the annual race to carry that valued commodity from China to London. Next, it was retrofitted to carry wool and won the annual wool race from Melbourne, Australia, to London every year between 1885 and 1895. In 1954, the ship was brought to Greenwich and designated a memorial to the Merchant Navy. In 2007, a fire gutted it, but an extensive restoration project has returned the clipper to its

GOOD **EATS**

■ **PLATEAU**
This stylish, fine-dining restaurant with great views of Canary Wharf serves flawless nouvelle French dishes **4th Floor, Canada Place, E14, tel 020 7715 7100, £££**

■ **MERAZ CAFÉ**
The restaurant serves a fusion of Indian, Bangladeshi, and Pakistani cooking known as Bharthian cuisine. **56 Hanbury St., E1, tel 020 7247 6999, £**

■ **TRAFALGAR TAVERN**
This popular pub beside the river was frequented by novelist Charles Dickens and Prime Minister William Gladstone. The restaurant serves modern British dishes. **6 Park Row, SE10, tel 020 3887 9886, £££**

former glory. The *Cutty Sark* stands beside the southern entrance to the Greenwich Foot Tunnel, which runs under the Thames to the Isle of Dogs on the north side of the river.

Greenwich Church St., SE10 • tel 020 8312 6565 • Closed Dec 25–26 • £££££ • DLR: Cutty Sark • rmg.co.uk

Old Royal Naval College

7 One of architect Sir Christopher Wren's masterpieces, this pair of elegant colonnaded buildings graces the riverbank at Greenwich. Built by Queen Mary II between 1696 and 1712 for injured and retired sailors, the hospital was converted into a staff college for naval officers in 1873. Military cutbacks forced its closure in the 1990s. Many of the buildings are now part of Greenwich University, but two areas are open to the public. The spectacular **Painted Hall,** named for the huge wall and ceiling paintings by James Thornhill, was planned as the hospital's dining hall, but was considered too grand. It remained empty until January 1806, when Admiral Lord Nelson, hero of the Battle of Trafalgar against Napoleon's fleet, lay in state here. The **chapel,** rebuilt in neoclassical style in 1789 after a fire, is the work of architect James Stuart.

Greenwich, SE10 • tel 020 8269 4747 • Closed Dec. 24–26 • £££ • DLR: Cutty Sark • ornc.org

National Maritime Museum

8 One of the world's largest maritime museums has a rich collection of maps, instruments, model ships, and souvenirs from all over the world. Nelson's jacket with the fatal hole made by a French musket ball at the Battle of Trafalgar is among its collection. Exhibits on three levels include four new galleries that regale guests with the adventures of **Tudor and Stuart Seafarers**, Arctic and Antarctic exploration in **Polar Worlds**, and voyages of discovery in the world's largest ocean in **Pacific Encounters**. Eclectic displays in the **Sea Things** gallery help visitors to explore how the ocean

EAST LONDON

has made us who we are, as individuals and societies. Children can navigate the world with the **Great Map**, one of many interactive displays.

Romney Rd., SE10 • tel 020 8858 4422 • Closed Dec. 24–26 • DLR: Cutty Sark • rmg.co.uk

Royal Observatory

9 Perched on the hill behind the National Maritime Museum, the Royal Observatory was founded in 1675 by King Charles II for research in navigation. On display are some of the world's first portable timepieces, which were used for navigation at sea. The most popular feature, located in the courtyard, is the **prime meridian**—0° longitude—which divides the world into East and West. At night, the Observatory projects a laser light into the sky along the meridian. The site also includes a **planetarium** with daily shows.

Blackheath Ave., SE10 • tel 020 8858 4422 • Closed Dec. 24–26 • DLR: Cutty Sark • £££ • rmg.co.uk

EAST LONDON

Stand astride the prime meridian with a foot in each hemisphere at the Royal Observatory.

Tower of London

*Fortress, royal residence, prison, and home to the Crown Jewels,
the medieval Tower has a long and at times bloody history.*

The Tower's round turret, second from right, contained the first royal observatory.

William the Conqueror ordered the construction of the Tower in the 11th century as a fortress. Successive kings altered and expanded it throughout the 12th and 13th centuries. During its 900-year history, it has been used as a royal home, an arsenal, a mint, and a menagerie—but it is probably most famous as a prison. Of the many "guests" kept here—including kings, queens, advisors, and former royal favorites—some were executed on Tower Green. The Yeoman Warders, or Beefeaters, act as guards and guides.

ROYAL ARMOR

The central stronghold, known as the **White Tower,** is the oldest part of the fortress. It houses an exhibition of royal armor, including a large decorative suit made for King Henry VIII in 1540 and a suit covered in gold leaf made in 1612 that belonged to King Charles I.

CROWN JEWELS

Among the dazzling array of 23,578 jewels on display in the **Jewel House** is **St. Edward's Crown,** decorated with sapphires, tourmalines, amethysts, topazes, and citrines, and last worn by Queen Elizabeth II at her coronation in 1953. The crown weighs an uncomfortable 4.9 pounds (2.22 kg), and many monarchs have declined to wear it, opting instead for the **Imperial State Crown,** which is decorated with 2,868 diamonds, 273 pearls, 17 sapphires, 11 emeralds, and five rubies.

FEATHERED GUARDIANS

Tower Green is the place to see the **ravens** that guard the tower. According to legend, if they ever left the Tower, the White Tower would collapse and disaster would engulf England. To ensure this never happened, King

SAVVY **TRAVELER**

Arrive at the Tower as early as possible in the morning, especially in the summer, since the lines grow quickly.

Charles II decreed that there must always be six ravens in residence.

TRAITORS' GATE

In the 13th century, King Edward I built a gate at river level beneath **St. Thomas's Tower** to provide access to the Tower by boat. In Tudor times, prisoners of the monarch—many of whom were accused of treason—arrived this way.

PRINCES IN THE TOWER

The **Bloody Tower** acquired its name in the 16th century because it was thought this was where Richard of Gloucester (later King Richard III) murdered his two nephews, Edward V and his brother Richard, in 1483. Two hundred years later, the skeletons of two boys were discovered here. A room houses an exhibition about their disappearance. Others imprisoned in the tower included Sir Walter Raleigh, a favorite of Queen Elizabeth I. A room is furnished as it might have been when he was here.

EAST LONDON

Tower of London, Tower Hill, EC3 • tel 020 3166 6000 • Closed Jan. 1 and Dec. 24–26 • £££££ • Tube: Tower Hill • hrp.org.uk/toweroflondon

Maritime City

For more than 200 years, London was at the heart of the world's most powerful maritime power. The Royal Navy enforced British rule across much of the globe, and British trading ships imported large quantities of tea, sugar, spices, tobacco, and a host of other commodities. By the 19th century, new warehouses, docks, and shipbuilding companies had transformed East London into the world's busiest port.

St. Katharine Docks (above) by Tower Bridge have been converted into a marina; in the early 20th century, the area around Tower Bridge (right) was a working port.

Roman Port

The Romans chose the stretch of riverbank between Tower Bridge and London Bridge for their new capital. The river here flowed wide and deep enough to take seagoing vessels, yet was narrow enough for the construction of a bridge—prerequisites for a successful inland port.

The World's Warehouse

Beginning in the 17th century, Britain's empire grew based on global trade, and the port of London expanded into the biggest ever known. By the 18th century, wharves and warehouses, with moorings for hundreds of ships, lined both banks, while a continuous parade of tall-masted ships thronged the river.

It was a chaotic, dangerous place. Crews from all corners of the world waited for their ships to be unloaded, and gangs of thieves prowled at night. Thousands of dockworkers were employed loading and unloading cargo, yet the port still could not meet the expanding demand from larger and more numerous ships. A solution was found in the early 19th century with the creation of the West India, East India, and Surrey Commercial Docks, among others. These walled, wet docks provided safe berths, efficient unloading, and better links to the industries of East London.

Decline & Rebirth

During World War II, more than 25,000 bombs fell on or around the docks. Some basins were repaired, others were filled in, and trade continued. Then, in the 1960s, the new container ships proved too large for the port's facilities and went elsewhere. Within 20 years, all the docks had closed. A huge revitalization program has seen the Docklands area emerge as a flourishing financial center, and soaring waterfront offices and glossy apartment buildings have created a new riverscape.

FLOATING **MUSEUM**

The most visible sign of the Royal Navy in London today is the cruiser **H.M.S. *Belfast*** (*Morgan's Lane, SE1, closed Dec. 24–26, £££££, iwm.org .uk*). The ship is one of the most powerful ever built for the Royal Navy. It saw service in World War II and Korea and was used for peacekeeping duties in the 1950s and '60s. Now it is moored on the Thames close to Tower Bridge and offers visitors a taste of life aboard a 20th-century warship.

Hip East London Shops

East London has some of Europe's hippest alternative shopping. While the city's West End has contemporary designers, the East has developed a taste for stylish clothes from yesteryear. In the boutiques around Brick Lane, you can pick up a classic 1940s dress for a fraction of the cost of a new design.

EAST LONDON

■ BEYOND RETRO

With vintage clothes such as 1960s blazers, 1940s dresses, and 1980s pantsuits, Beyond Retro prides itself on finding the best 20th-century fashion. With a wide range of clothing on offer, you should be able to find something that appeals to you, and with prices at around £30 ($48) for a dress, a purchase won't break the bank.

110–112 Cheshire St., E2 • tel 020 7729 9001 • Closed Dec. 25–26 • Tube: Liverpool Street • beyondretro.com

■ VINTAGE BASEMENT

Unique items from the 1950s through the 1980s fill the racks of this shop. It's fun to browse through the vintage clothing—and if you do make a purchase, you're unlikely to see anyone else wearing the same outfit.

7 Cheshire St., E2 • tel 020 7729 2908 • Closed Dec. 25 • Tube: Liverpool Street • facebook.com/vintagebasementbricklane

■ INSPITALFIELDS

Unusual designer items for the home, including some with a London theme, fill a series of rooms. Stock ranges from well-known brands to hand-made designs from local artists and is constantly changing. The store started out as a market stall in Old Spitalfields Market, which is still one of the liveliest scenes in East London (at its busiest on Thursday to Sunday).

13 Lamb St., E1 • tel 020 7247 2477 • Tube: Liverpool Street or Aldgate East • oldspitalfieldsmarket.com

■ HOSTEM

Redchurch Street is known for its art galleries and high-end stores such as Hostem, which sells handmade suits and garments for the "true sartorialist" from selected designers. Check out the handiwork of top English designers such as Casely-Hayford and Margaret Howell. See

Head to Redchurch Street for interesting one-off clothing and shoe stores.

why handmade shoes by Sebastian Tarek cost around £1,000 (he makes just 24 pairs a year). The store also sells cashmere sweaters and high-end luggage. Visit the basement to see the full range.

28 Old Nichol St., E2 • tel 020 7729 4098 • Closed Sun.–Tues. • Tube: Shoreditch • hostem. co.uk

■ WALCONCEPT

Among the stalls at Old Spitalfields, this gem stands out for its curated vintage clothing, including genuine WWII-era sheepskin bomber jackets.

Flawlessly dressed owner Waliou also has a great stock of retro scarves, cravats and ties.

13 Lamb St., E1 • tel 020 7247 2477 • Closed Thur. • Tube: Liverpool Street or Aldgate East • oldspitalfieldsmarket.com

■ VINYL PIMP

From Motown classics to techno, its vast collection makes this the go-to shop for yesteryear vinyl discs, including sets from top DJs such as Ray Keith.

14 Felstead St., E9 • tel 020 8985 2127 • Tube: Liverpool Street • vinylpimp.co.uk

PART 3

Travel Essentials

PLANNING YOUR TRIP

When to Go

January, February, and **March** are good months for getting into popular plays and operas, and enjoying museums without the long lines. For sports, there are plenty of soccer and rugby matches, and the Oxford vs. Cambridge boat race takes place on the Thames. Daffodils carpet the lawns of the parks, while trees burst into leaf.

April and **May** mark an increase in events, such as arts festivals, houses that open only for the summer months, the culmination of the soccer season, the start of the cricket season, and the popular Chelsea Flower Show.

June brings the summer-long season of open-air concerts at Kenwood House and Marble Hill House and the All England Lawn Tennis Championships at Wimbledon. Ceremonial events peak, too, with Beating Retreat and Trooping the Colour.

July and **August** are when museums and theaters fill up with visitors. Cultural highlights include the nightly Henry Wood Promenade ("The Proms") concerts at the Royal Albert Hall. Cricket continues through the summer, and you can enjoy open-air theater in Regent's Park and open-air concerts at Kenwood House on the edge of Hampstead Heath.

September and **October** mix festivals on the Thames and in Covent Garden with major art shows, operas, and plays. In the parks, sunny days bring the crowds, especially on weekends and public holidays.

November and **December** are strong on festivities: Shops and streets are decorated for the holidays, theater tickets need to be reserved in advance, and an abundance of music is performed in concert halls, cathedrals, and churches.

Climate

British weather can be a daily surprise, and a sunny morning can become a wet afternoon. Be prepared and carry a fold-up umbrella and consider waterproof shoes.

Passports & Visas

Nationals of the United States, Canada, Australia, and New Zealand can enter the United Kingdom with just a passport.

HOW TO GET TO CENTRAL LONDON

From the Airports

Gatwick (tel 0844 892 0322, gatwickairport.com) lies 30 miles (48 km) south of central London. The Gatwick Express (tel 0345 850 1530, gatwickexpress.com) train runs to Victoria, a 30-minute ride, every 15 minutes by day and less frequently by night. By road, the Easybus (easybus.co.uk) takes around 70 minutes and departs about every 20 minutes, 24 hours a day. Taking a taxi costs more than £60 ($90).

Heathrow (tel 0844 351 801, heathrowairport.com) is the city's main airport, 15 miles (24 km) west of central London. By rail, the Heathrow Express (tel 0345 600 1515, heathrowexpress.com) to Paddington, a 20-minute ride, runs every 15 minutes between 5:12 a.m. and 11:42 p.m. By Tube, the Piccadilly line, a 60-minute ride, runs regularly from 5:02 a.m. to 11:42 a.m. through central London. On Fri. and Sat., there is a 24-hour service from Terminal 5. National Express (tel 08717 818 181, nationalexpress.com) buses go to Victoria Coach Station about every 30 minutes and take 60 to 90 minutes. Taking a taxi costs around £60 ($90).

London City Airport (tel 020 7646 0088, londoncityairport.com) is a small airport 9 miles (14 km) east of central London. It has a Docklands Light Railway station with links to Canary Wharf and Bank, both on the Tube and DLR.

Stansted (tel 0844 335 1803, stanstedairport.com) is 35 miles (56 km) northeast of central London; travel by rail is faster than road. Stansted Express (stanstedexpress.com) to Liverpool Street station takes 42 minutes and runs every 15 minutes between 5:30 a.m. and 12:30 a.m.

By Train or Bus

Eurostar trains *(eurostar .com)* arrive at St. Pancras International *(tel 020 7843 7688, stpancras.com)* from Paris, Disneyland Paris, Brussels, and Lille.

National trains *(tel 03457 484 950, nationalrail.co.uk)* service Charing Cross, Euston, King's Cross, Liverpool Street, Paddington, St. Pancras, Victoria, and Waterloo terminals.

Long-distance bus services arrive at Victoria Coach Station. National Express *(tel 08717 818 181, nationalexpress.com)* is Britain's biggest bus company, and also travels to the Netherlands, Belgium, France, and Ireland.

GETTING AROUND

London Transportation

Taxis, although fun, are just one transportation experience, and the costs mount up very quickly. Take the Tube or a bus, and if you are lost, just ask for directions. Transport for London *(tel 0343 222 1234, tfl.gov.uk)* runs an excellent journey planner on its website, offering the quickest and easiest way to complete your journey.

Taxi

There are two kinds of taxis: the "black cab" and the minicab. Black cab drivers have all passed "The Knowledge" exams and know the city extremely well. To use one,

either go to a taxi stand, call a company such as Radio Taxis *(tel 020 7272 0272, gett.com/uk)*, or hail one on the street. Minicabs may have uninsured cars.

Mass Transit

Underground fares are structured according to nine zones, while buses charge per journey. Tickets can be bought for each individual trip, or you can buy a Travelcard, but the most economical way is an Oyster card *(oyster.tfl.gov.uk)*. These can be bought at any Tube/DLR station for a deposit of £5 ($7.80). Load money onto the card at the ticket office or touchscreen machines, and touch the card on the yellow disks at ticket barriers at the start and the conclusion of your journey. For buses, only touch on entry. Oyster card fares are less than other fares.

Bus

There is nothing quite like rumbling through London on a bus, looking at the people, buildings, advertisements, and street art. All bus stops have maps showing bus routes and nearby stops. Pay with an Oyster card or Travelcard. Cash is not accepted.

Tube (Underground)

This huge system of a dozen lines and 270 stations snakes all over London and carries 2.5 million people a day. London's Tube (subway) is well lit, easy to use, and safe. First, plot your route on the Tube

map. Then, buy a Travelcard, Oyster card, or individual ticket. Use this to pass through the automatic barriers, get on the correct color-coded line, and ensure you are traveling in the right direction. To change lines, follow the signs to the connecting line on the platform. Use your ticket or card to exit through the barriers. When in doubt, ask; Londoners get lost too.

Bike

Pay £2 ($3) for 24-hour access to release-codes for the many Santander bike stands dotted around the city, either at the stand, online, or by phone *(tel 0343 222 6666, tfl.gov. uk)*. Journeys cost £2 for each 30 minutes thereafter. When you're finished, lock the bike back into its stand at any of 750 docking stations.

Docklands Light Railway (DLR)

This high-level railway *(tel 0343 222 1234, tfl.gov.uk/ modes/dlr)* runs from Bank and Tower Gateway stations, and on through Docklands and East London.

Organized Sightseeing

Even the most independent traveler may wish to take a tour sometimes. Bus tours give an overview of the city, walking tours open your eyes to a street's history, river tours provide a new perspective, and some tours get you into places usually closed to the public.

TRAVEL **ESSENTIALS**

Bus Tours

Big Bus Company *(tel 020 7808 6753, bigbustours.com)*; **Original London Sightseeing Tour** *(tel 020 8877 1722, theoriginaltour.com)*; and **City Tours London** *(tel 020 3950 1262, london.city-tour.com)*, which has hop-on/hop-off bus tours.

River Tours

The best website for boat tours is *tfl.gov.uk.*

Tailor-made Tours

For a guide with the highest qualifications, the Blue Badge, contact **Tour Guides** *(tel 020 7611 2545, guidelondon.org.uk)*, which offers a wide range of specialist tours covering London from every angle.

Walking Tours

Guided Walks and Tours *(tel 020 7606 3030, cityoflondon .gov.uk)*; **London Walks** *(tel 020 7624 3978, www.walks. com)* has a huge variety of walks led by enthusiasts.

PRACTICAL ADVICE

Electricity

The supply is 230V, with a permitted range of 216.2–253V, and 50 Hz. Plugs are three-pin, type G. U.S. appliances need a voltage transformer and an adapter.

Money Matters

Sterling currency is used throughout Britain: 100 pence make 1 pound. Coins are in denominations of 1p, 2p, 5p, 10p, 20p, 50p, £1, and £2. Notes are in £5, £10, £20, and £50.

What's Going On?

Time Out (timeout.com), published on Tuesdays and distributed free, provides lists of London activities, together with reviews and previews. Quality newspapers include the *Daily Telegraph*, the *Financial Times*, and the *Guardian*; London's only evening paper is the free *Evening Standard*, daily Monday to Friday. The *Metro* is a free morning tabloid, widely available at Tube stations.

Opening Hours

Shops are open seven days a week, but many limit opening hours on Sundays. Late night shopping takes place on Wednesday (Knightsbridge) and Thursday (Oxford St., Regent St., and Covent Garden). Banks open Monday to Friday from 9:30 a.m. to 4:30 p.m. Chequepoint branches at 24 Wardour Street open 24 hours.

Post Offices

Stamps can be bought at post offices and some newsstands and shops.

Public Holidays

January 1, Good Friday, Easter Monday, first Monday in May, last Monday in May, last Monday in August, December 25 and 26. If you're traveling across the country on any of these days, expect delays.

Restrooms

Otherwise known as toilets, lavatories, loos, WCs, ladies, and gents. If the public restrooms are unsavory, slip into the nearest large department store or hotel.

Smoking

Smoking is prohibited in all bars, pubs, restaurants, and other enclosed public places.

Telephones

The city code for London is 020. (When calling from the U.S., omit the initial "0.") To make a call within London, either use coins or use your credit card. Omit the 020 city code and dial the eight-digit number. Outside London, numbers usually have a three- or five-digit code and a six-figure number. Non-geographical numbers beginning 0845, 0870, or similar are charged higher rates.

The London Pass

This is a bargain way of visiting several of London's fee-paying attractions *(tel 020 7293 0972, londonpass.com)*.

Time Differences

GMT (Greenwich Mean Time) is standard time; BST (British Summer Time) is one hour ahead of GMT and runs from late March to late October. GMT is five hours ahead of U.S. Eastern Standard Time.

Tourist Information

There are no tourist offices open to the public in the U.S.

or Canada. All information is online at visitbritain.com.

Useful Websites

a-zmaps.co.uk
For a range of useful maps
bbc.co.uk/london For news, travel, weather, entertainment, and sports
cityoflondon.gov.uk
Official City of London website, has lots of useful information
londonist.com
All-encompassing visitor information
londonnet.co.uk
Restaurants, bars, and nightlife
londontown.com
Basic information on top sights, hotels, etc.
officiallondontheatre.co.uk
On-the-day information on half-price theater tickets
riverthames.co.uk
Places and events on the river
streetmap.co.uk
Plan your day, then print out the street plan
tfl.gov.uk
For all transport
ticketmaster.co.uk
For tickets to events
timeout.com
For all event listings
visitbritain.com
The British Tourist Board
visitlondon.com
The London Tourist Board

Visitors with Disabilities

Facilities are generally good for visitors with disabilities. Artsline (disabilityarts.online) has advice on access to entertainment and arts venues. RADAR (the Royal Society for Disability and Rehabilitation)

provides information on tour operators that cater specifically to disabled travelers (tel 0330 995 0400, disabilityrights.uk.org).

EMERGENCIES

Police, Fire, & Ambulance

To summon any of these emergency services, dial 999 from any telephone, free of charge.

Lost Property

Always inform the police to validate insurance claims. Report a lost passport to your embassy. For lost property on the Tube, buses, black taxi cabs, and London Overground, contact Transport for London Lost Property Office (200 Baker St., NW1, tel 0343 222 1234, Mon– Fri. 8:30 a.m.–4 p.m., tfl.gov.uk). Property lost on the DLR is held for 48 hours at Poplar Station (tel 020 7363 9550) and then forwarded to the office at 200 Baker St. (above).

Health Precautions

If you need a doctor or dentist, ask your hotel reception for advice. If the problem is minor go to the nearest chemist (pharmacy) and speak to the pharmacist. For insurance claims, keep receipts for all treatments and medicines.

National Health Service (N.H.S.) Hospitals

Hospitals with 24-hour emergency departments include:
Chelsea and Westminster Hospital (369 Fulham Rd.,

SW10, tel 020 8746 8000)
University College Hospital (Gower St., entrance in Grafton Way, WC1, tel 020 3456 7890).

Other Facilities

For an optician and on-site repair workshop, try **Eyeworks London** (44 Gloucester Rd., SW7, tel 020 7584 2697). Those with more serious eye problems should seek help at **Moorfields Eye Hospital** (City Rd., EC1, tel 020 7253 3411).

Chemists (Pharmacies)

Many drugs freely available in the U.S. cannot be bought over the counter in the UK. Be sure to bring sufficient supplies of medicines from home. If more are needed, take the wrapping with a full printed description of its contents to the chemist for advice on purchasing the nearest equivalent. Chemists that open from 9 a.m. until midnight include **Bliss Chemist** (5 Marble Arch, W1, tel 020 7723 6116). **Zafash Chemists** (233 Old Brompton Rd., SW5, tel 020 7373 2798) is open 24 hours.

Embassies & Consulates

Canadian High Commission, 1 Grosvenor Sq., W1, tel 020 7004 6000, canadainternational.gc.ca
Embassy of the United States of America, 33 Nine Elms Ln., SW11, tel 020 7499 9000, uk.usembassy.gov.

HOTELS

Location is the key to a successful London visit. There are hotels of every level of luxury, from simple to exotic, but their location is paramount: London is very big; hours—and money—can be wasted moving around. You must also be aware of your budget. Sleeping in London is expensive—the average room in London costs around $150 a night, but the high-end hotels can charge many times more. It is wise to figure out where you will be spending your days and evenings, then choose a well-placed hotel that suits your lifestyle, plans, and budget. And be sure to plan ahead—London has plenty of hotel rooms, but the best get booked up in advance.

Every month new hotels open in London, to add to its collection of well-worn favorites. They span all price brackets, from the luxurious to the basic, but the emphasis is on design-led hotels, such as Kit Kemp's Firmdale hotels, including The Soho with its fashionable bar. Myhotel, which opened in Chelsea in late 1998, was Terence Conran's first hotel, planned with a feng shui expert as an "oasis of calm." Subsequently, he lavishly transformed the Great Eastern Hotel (now the Andaz) in the City. Ian Schrager and Philippe Starck have brought New York panache and success to London with new hotels, including the Sanderson and St. Martin's Lane.

Boutique hotels have long been established in South Kensington with such successes as The Gore. Up-scale choices spread across central London—to Hazlitt's in Soho, Charlotte Street in Fitzrovia, the Rookery in Clerkenwell, and Threadneedles in the City.

More traditional luxury hotels, such as the Ritz, Savoy, Berkeley, Claridge's, and Dorchester, have been joined by the Mandarin Oriental group's Hyde Park Hotel. Other refurbished hotels include Le Méridien Piccadilly and the St. Pancras Renaissance, while a number of the city's protected historic buildings have been converted to hotel use, such as the Rosewood and The Royal Horseguards Hotel.

It is important to make reservations well in advance. And try to save money by asking about special deals when making a reservation. These may include weekends or during the quiet month of February, when you may find a better deal at a deluxe hotel than at a popular business hotel. New hotels often offer discounts while they deal with teething troubles. Some hotels have economic family rooms; others, such as the Citadines London Trafalgar Square, have a kitchen in each room.

When reserving, you may be asked for a deposit or for your credit card number. Check the room rate carefully: It should include the 20 percent VAT tax, but occasionally prices are given without it.

If anything goes wrong during your stay, talk to the duty manager. If the problem isn't resolved, talk to the manager, then put it in writing.

Visit London has a hotel information and reservation section on its website (visitlondon .com) and publishes the reliable booklet "Where to Stay & What to Do." It also handles serious complaints.

Some of the nicest hotels are in old buildings that may not have all the modern conveniences. If you have particular needs in comfort, services, or anything else, check that your hotel can provide them before you book.

Visitors with disabilities can obtain information on suitable places to stay from **Tourism for All** (1 Pixel Mill, 44 Appleby Rd., Kendal, Cumbria LA9 6ES, tel 0845 124 9971, or 0044 1539 726 111 for calls from outside the UK, tourismforall.org.uk).

Apartments

Those visiting for longer periods may wish to rent a serviced apartment on a weekly basis. Rates can be very competitive even in the city center. Agencies specializing in vacation rentals include **Coach House Rentals** (tel 020 8355 3192, *chsrentals.com*). **The King's Wardrobe** *(tel 020 7792 2222, bridgestreet.co.uk)* has modest, well-priced apartments near St. Paul's Cathedral. **No. 5 Maddox Street** *(tel 020 7647 0200, living-rooms.co.uk)* has suites equipped with workstations, balconies, and minimalist decor. **Citadines London Trafalgar Square** *(tel 0800 376 3898, citadines. com)* has 187 simple studios and one- and two-bedroom apartments in an unbeatable location. Citadines also has properties in Barbican, Holborn, Mayfair, and South Kensington.

Organization
Hotels listed here have been grouped first according to neighborhood, then listed alphabetically by price range.

Price Range
An indication of the cost of a double room in the high season is given by **£** signs.

£££££	Over £275
££££	£201–£275
£££	£151–£200
££	£75–£150
£	Under £75

Text Symbols
(I) *No. of Guest Rooms*
🚇 *Tube*

THE CITY
London's historic heart has some hotels whose elegance matches their history.

■ Andaz
£££££
40 LIVERPOOL STREET EC2
TEL 020 7961 1234
andaz.hyatt.com
Conran took a grand Victorian railroad station and stylishly transformed it into a modern City hotel, though now renamed and run by Hyatt.
(I) *267* 🚇 *Liverpool Street*

■ Threadneedles
£££££
5 THREADNEEDLE STREET EC2
TEL 020 7657 8080
hotelthreadneedles.co.uk
The City's original boutique hotel is inside a fine former Midland Bank building. The diverse yet equally elegant rooms are equipped with plasma TVs and other gadgets.
(I) *69* 🚇 *Bank*

■ Rookery
££££
12 PETER'S LANE, COWCROSS STREET EC1
TEL 020 7336 0931
rookeryhotel.com
Lavish and tasteful rooms with sumptuous period furnishings in Georgian row houses are under the same management as the successful Hazlitt's (see p. 183).
(I) *33* 🚇 *Farringdon*

WESTMINSTER
At the heart of London, close to many key sights,

the capital's grandest hotels have exceptional restaurants and lively bars, which make excellent rendezvous spots.

■ The Athenaeum
£££££
116 PICCADILLY W1
TEL 020 7499 3464
athenaeumhotel.com
The elegant comfort and high level of service draw guests back to the Athenaeum's rooms and apartments, as do Windsor Lounge teas and the spa. Higher rooms have park views.
(I) *156* 🚇 *Hyde Park Corner*

■ Brown's
£££££
ALBEMARLE STREET W1
TEL 020 7493 6020
roccofortehotels.com
Traditional English elegance in the heart of old Mayfair, brought right up to date. Roaring fires and creaking floorboards are an echo of Mayfair mansions. Fine dining, and especially good traditional tea.
(I) *117* 🚇 *Green Park*

■ Claridge's
£££££
BROOK STREET W1
TEL 020 7629 8860
claridges.co.uk
The queen's state guests move here after Buckingham Palace. It has huge corner suites. The glorious public rooms include the grand dining room—design by Thierry Despont and Diane von Furstenberg, food by Daniel Humm.
(I) *203* 🚇 *Bond Street*

HOTELS

TRAVEL ESSENTIALS

■ The Connaught
££££££
CARLOS PLACE W1
TEL 020 7499 7070
the-connaught.co.uk
In this most discreet of London hotels the famous can remain anonymous. Recently refurbished, it boasts two-Michelin-star food from Hélène Darroze and two fine bars, the Coburg and Connaught.
ⓘ 122 🚇 Bond Street

■ The Dorchester
££££££
43 PARK LANE W1
TEL 020 7898 9880
thedorchester.com
Lavishly furnished, including the rooftop Oliver Messel rooms and a luscious spa. Guests and visitors can enjoy fine Promenade teas, a buzzy bar, and restaurants: the traditional Grill, three-Michelin-star Alain Ducasse, and opulent China Tang (Cantonese), plus traditional afternoon tea.
ⓘ 250 🚇 Hyde Park Corner

■ Four Seasons
££££££
HAMILTON PLACE
PARK LANE W1
TEL 020 7499 0888
fourseasons.com/london
Recently smartly restyled, this is an intelligently designed hotel with excellent rooms and suites; some of London's top chefs have worked in the Four Seasons' restaurant (modern European).
ⓘ 192 🚇 Hyde Park Corner

■ Landmark Hotel
££££££
222 MARYLEBONE ROAD NW1
TEL 020 7631 8000
landmarklondon.co.uk
The spectacular Winter Garden, a palm court that operates all day, sets the tone for this grand late-Victorian building. It has large rooms with good bathrooms, and is surprisingly well-located.
ⓘ 300 🚇 Marylebone

■ Le Méridien Piccadilly
££££££
21 PICCADILLY W1
TEL 020 7734 8000
lemeridienpiccadilly.co.uk
Located at the crossroads of St. James's, Mayfair, and theaterland. Guests enjoy fine rooms in black, white, and red, plus a splendid health club and spa, afternoon tea in the Oak Room, and excellent bars.
ⓘ 266 🚇 Piccadilly Circus

■ Metropolitan
££££££
19 OLD PARK LANE W1
TEL 020 7447 1000
comohotels.com
The Metropolitan has a reputation for cutting-edge design and matching guests checking into its rooms and apartments. Getting a reservation at its Nobu restaurant (Japanese) is hard, but it also has the new Gridiron live-fire grill, plus a Shambhala spa.
ⓘ 150 🚇 Hyde Park Corner

■ The Ritz
££££££
150 PICCADILLY W1
TEL 020 7493 8181
theritzlondon.com
Exquisite hotel overlooking Green Park, whose painted-and-gilded dining room is London's most beautiful. The bar is a promenade for the stylish, and the new Secret Garden Bar is open in spring and summer. No jeans or sneakers, and men must wear jacket and tie.
ⓘ 136 🚇 Green Park

■ The Royal Horseguards
££££££
2 WHITEHALL COURT SW1
TEL 020 7523 5062
guoman.com
Ideally located, this grand Victorian Thames-side building was once home to the secret service and the military. Afternoon teas are a high spot.
ⓘ 281 🚇 Charing Cross

■ The Stafford
££££££
16–18 ST. JAMES'S PLACE SW1
TEL 020 7493 0111
thestaffordlondon.com
One of London's most luxurious small hotels, tucked down an alley off St. James's Street, it re-creates Victorian style. There is a delightful dining room and fine wines stored in 350-year-old cellars.
ⓘ 105 🚇 Green Park

■ The Trafalgar Hotel
££££££
2 SPRING GARDENS W1
TEL 020 7870 2900
thetrafalgar.com
Designed to attract younger guests, this lifestyle hotel

has sharp service, good design, and the popular Rockwell Bar and summer rooftop bar overlooking Trafalgar Square.

🄸 129 🄰 Charing Cross

■ Durrants Hotel

££££
26–32 GEORGE STREET W1
TEL 020 7935 8131
durrantshotel.co.uk

This quiet and respectful Georgian-era hotel opened in 1790, and descendants of the original family maintain its comfortable tone today.

🄸 92 🄰 Bond Street

SOUTH BANK

The strip along the south bank of the Thames is one of the city's most exciting and innovative areas.

■ London Marriott County Hall

£££££
COUNTY HALL, WESTMINSTER BRIDGE ROAD SE1
TEL 020 7928 5200
marriott.co.uk

This newly refurbished hotel is in part of the old riverside London County Hall building. Some rooms have river views, and the leisure facilities, including a pool, are first class.

🄸 200 🄰 Westminster/Waterloo

■ Sea Containers London

£££–£££££
20 UPPER GROUND SE1
TEL 020 3747 1000
seacontainerslondon.com

This über-smart riverside hotel in Sea Containers House near Blackfriars Bridge is inspired by

the building's nautical history. It is as close as it gets to the river.

🄸 359 🄰 Blackfriars

■ Mad Hatter

££££
3–7 STAMFORD STREET SE1
TEL 020 7401 9222
madhatterhotel.com

A brewery-run pub and hotel in a former hat factory, a couple of blocks back from the river between Tate Modern and South Bank Centre.

🄸 30 🄰 Blackfriars

■ Premier Inn

££
85 YORK ROAD SE1
TEL 0871 527 8648
premierinn.com

This no-frills, good value hotel behind the deluxe London Marriott has an excellent location close to Waterloo Station. No river views.

🄸 313 🄰 Westminster/Waterloo

TRAFALGAR SQUARE & SOHO

The heart of the city, Trafalgar Square is close to many of London's major attractions, many of its theaters, and Soho's vibrant nightlife.

■ St. Martin's Lane

£££££
45 ST. MARTIN'S LANE WC2
TEL 020 7300 5500
stmartinslane.com

Hovering between West End theaters and Covent Garden restaurants, Philippe Starck's dramatically minimalist rooms and extensive bars attract design-conscious clients.

🄸 204 🄰 Covent Garden/Leicester Square

■ Dean Street Townhouse

££££
71 DEAN STREET W1
TEL 020 7434 1775
deanstreettownhouse.com

This chic Soho hotel opened in a converted four-story Georgian town house with a rich history. Public spaces are opulent, while the rooms have original features and a decorative palette of mostly soft browns and off-whites. The popular dining room with an outside patio (open to nonpatrons) has a traditional, clublike atmosphere, and servesclassic British food.

🄸 39 🄰 Tottenham Court Road

■ Hazlitt's

££££
6 FRITH STREET W1
TEL 020 7434 1771
hazlittshotel.com

Combining three Georgian town houses, one once the home of writer William Hazlitt (1778–1830), this gracious hotel is in the heart of Soho. There are antiques in the beautifully furnished rooms. Ideal for theater and museum visits. As this is a landmark hotel, there are no elevators. There is minimal room service.

🄸 30 🄰 Tottenham Court Road

■ The Soho Hotel

££££
4 RICHMOND MEWS
DEAN STREET W1
TEL 020 7559 3000
firmdale.com

Designer Kit Kemp's sixth London hotel (see *firmdale.com*

for the others) mixes country style with urban simplicity in a bare brick building. Lovely bathrooms and a buzzing bar and restaurant.

🛈 91 **🚇** *Tottenham Court Road*

■ Sanctum Soho Hotel
££££
20 WARWICK STREET W1
TEL 020 7292 6100
sanctumsoho.com
This superbly furnished minimalistic hotel spreads overtwo Georgian town houses. It has a great location close to Regent Street and a rooftop garden terrace and bar.

🛈 30 **🚇** *Piccadilly Circus*

COVENT GARDEN TO LUDGATE HILL
Hotels range from grand to bargain in this superb location in the heart of London.

■ One Aldwych
£££££
1 ALDWYCH WC2
TEL 020 7300 1000
onealdwych.com
This newly refurbished hotel is one of London's most dynamic contemporary renovations. Built in 1907 for the long-since-gone *Morning Post* newspaper, One Aldwych has been transformed by Gordon Campbell-Gray and Mary Fox Linton into a state-of-the-art hotel. There is serious art on the walls, and a sumptuous and extensive health spa. Dining options include Indigo restaurant and the more formal adjoining Eneko Basque restaurant.

🛈 105 **🚇** *Charing Cross*

■ Rosewood
£££££
252 HIGH HOLBORN, WC1
TEL 020 7781
rosewoodhotels.com
Approached through a courtyard, this grand 1914 former insurance company building is a class act. Scarfes Bar, with live jazz, is decorated with cartoons by political satirist Gerald Scarfe.

🛈 262 **🚇** *Holborn*

■ The Savoy
£££££
STRAND WC2
TEL 020 7836 4343
thesavoylondon.com
One of London's most famous hotels is in an ideal stylish location for mixing City with West End, and sets the benchmark for deluxe elegance and service. The American Bar, Thames Foyer teas, and Kaspar's at The Savoy restaurant are all top-notch.

🛈 267 **🚇** *Charing Cross*

■ Covent Garden Hotel
££££
10 MONMOUTH STREET WC2
TEL 020 7806 1000
firmdale.com
The wood-paneled drawing room and atmospheric Tiffany's Library, together with the individualized, brightly colored rooms, make this hotel seem far from urban London's hub, despite its cinema.

🛈 58 **🚇** *Covent Garden*

■ Crowne Plaza London—The City
££££
19 NEW BRIDGE STREET EC4
TEL 0871 942 9190
cplondoncityhotel.co.uk
Located between Ludgate Hill and Fleet Street, and with a vibrant bar and the excellent Diciannove restaurant, this hotel is the perfect choice for exploring the city.

🛈 203 **🚇** *Blackfriars*

■ Haymarket Hotel
££££
1 SUFFOLK PLACE SW1
TEL 020 7470 4000
firmdale.com
One of the Firmdale group's stable of excellent, intimate hotels, located in the Haymarket at the heart of the theater district. Rooms are calm, quiet, and comfortable, and facilities include a gym and swimming pool. The hotel also offers pampering treatments.

🛈 50 **🚇** *Piccadilly Circus/ Leicester Square*

■ The Fielding Hotel
££
4 BROAD COURT, BOW STREET WC2
TEL 020 7836 8305
thefieldinghotel.co.uk
Quiet, simple accommodations, some with clawfoot tubs, in a pedestrian lane across from Covent Garden Opera.

🛈 25 **🚇** *Covent Garden*

BLOOMSBURY
This area has a full range of good hotels, all within walking distance of the Bloomsbury

museums, Covent Garden, and West End theaters.

■ Charlotte Street Hotel
££££
15–17 CHARLOTTE STREET WC1
TEL 020 7806 2000
firmdale.com
This is a smart yet friendly and relaxed hotel inside a period building on a buzzing street between Bloomsbury and the West End. It has a small gym, the reliable Oscar restaurant, plus a screening room for rainy days.
🚇 52 🚈 Tottenham Court Road

■ The Montague on the Gardens
££££
15 MONTAGUE STREET WC1
TEL 020 7637 1001
montaguehotel.com
Centrally located, this stylish hotel is imaginatively decorated, with attention to detail. Rooms offer bold decor and quality furnishings, while facilities include a leafy terrace bar with live music in summer.
🚇 100 🚈 Holborn

■ St. Pancras Renaissance
££££
EUSTON ROAD NW1
TEL 020 7841 3540
stpancraslondon.com
The Midland Grand Hotel in St. Pancras Station was London's premier station-hotel before it closed in 1935. Now fully refurbished, it has been brought back to life as a timeless terminus treasure with a stellar bar and restaurants.
🚇 245 🚈 King's Cross St. Pancras

■ Sanderson
££££
50 BERNERS STREET W1
TEL 020 7300 1400
sandersonlondon.com
As with its sister hotel, St. Martin's Lane (see p. 183), the Schrager-Starck partnership creates minimalist rooms and busy public spaces such as the Long Bar and terrace for the Mad Hatters Afternoon Tea.
🚇 150 🚈 Oxford Circus

■ Academy
£££
21 GOWER STREET WC1
TEL 020 7631 4115
theacademyhotel.co.uk
Set in five Georgian row houses, with opulent furnishings and discreet art, this fairy-tale view of English interiors works well.
🚇 50 🚈 Goodge Street

■ The Harlingford
££
61–63 CARTWRIGHT GARDENS WC1
TEL 020 7387 1551
harlingfordhotel.com
Despite the budget rates, all guests enjoy en-suite bathrooms decorated in a contemporary style. The management is friendly, and there is an adjacent garden and even a tennis court.
🚇 44 🚈 Russell Square/Euston

■ Morgan Hotel
££
24 BLOOMSBURY WC1
TEL 020 7636 3735
morganhotel.co.uk
Superbly located, this modest and good-value family-run hotel in twin Georgian houses near the British Museum has both rooms and small apartments.
🚇 17 🚈 Tottenham Court Road

■ Generator
£
37 TAVISTOCK PLACE WC1
TEL 020 7388 7666
generatorhostels.com
Steel, chrome, and exposed pipes—plus its huge size, lively bar, and Internet room- keep the setting sleek, the prices low, and the guests hip and happy. Dorm-style rooms and twins.
🚇 848 beds 🚈 Russell Square

KENSINGTON & SOUTH KENSINGTON

There are several town-house hotels in this residential area close to Hyde Park and some excellent museums.

■ Baglioni
£££££
60 HYDE PARK GATE SW7
TEL 020 7368 5700
baglionihotels.com
Inside a Victorian mansion opposite Kensington Palace, its atmosphere is easy, the decor chic modern, the rooms equipped with everything including espresso machines. There is a serious spa.
🚇 68 🚈 High Street Kensington

■ The Exhibitionist
££££
8–10 QUEENSBERRY PLACE SW7
TEL 020 7915 0000
theexhibitionisthotel.com
A suave 5-star boutique hotel, and companion to the nearby

HOTELS

Gainsborough, in the town houses of the former Gallery Hotel. Endearingly colorful rooms and personalized service are key draws.

(i) 37 🚇 *South Kensington*

■ The Gore
££££
190 QUEEN'S GATE SW7
TEL 020 7584 6601
gorehotel.com
Opened more than a century ago, the Gore carefully preserves its Victorian details with paneled rooms, potted ferns, rugs, and glorious stained-glass windows. The same building houses the excellent Bar 190 and 190 Queen's Gate (*tel 020 7584 6601*).

(i) 50 🚇 *South Kensington*

■ Aster House
£££
3 SUMNER PLACE SW7
TEL 020 7581 5888
asterhouse.com
This welcoming bed-and-breakfast has excellent service, attention to detail, a garden with a duck pond, and a delightful, plant-filled conservatory for breakfast.

(i) 13 🚇 *South Kensington*

■ The Mayflower Hotel
££-£££
26–28 TREBOVIR ROAD SW5
TEL 020 7370 0991
mayflowerhotel.co.uk
This hotel includes modern, well-appointed although small rooms, with a touch of the exotic, such as colonial ceiling fans. It also has adjoining apartments. Nearby are two sister hotels: Twenty Nevern

Square Hotel and New Linden Hotel.

(i) 48 🚇 *Earl's Court*

■ The Sumner
£££
54 UPPER BERKELEY STREET
MARBLE ARCH W1
TEL 020 7723 2244
thesumner.com
The much-loved 5 Sumner Place hotel in South Kensington now has a grander sister in this refurbished and elegant luxury town-house hotel in Marylebone.

(i) 20 🚇 *Marble Arch*

■ The Rushmore Hotel
££
11 TREBOVIR ROAD SW5
TEL 020 7370 3839
rushmore-hotel.co.uk
Frescoed walls, draped beds, an elegant breakfast room, and good service make this hotel a bargain deal. Handily just steps from the tube.

(i) 22 🚇 *Earl's Court*

CHELSEA, BELGRAVIA, & KNIGHTSBRIDGE
Stylish Londoners and foreign diplomats set the tone in one of London's plushest neighborhoods, with some discreet hotels.

■ The Berkeley
£££££
WILTON PLACE SW1
TEL 020 7235 6000
the-berkeley.co.uk
The Berkeley is a modern hotel run on traditional lines: open fire in the lobby, lavish

flowers, spacious rooms and signature suites, valet service. Excellent top-floor health club and pool are equaled by the bar and restaurants that include Marcus Wareing's Michelin-starred Marcus.

(i) 214 🚇 *Hyde Park Corner*

■ The Capital
£££££
22 BASIL STREET
KNIGHTSBRIDGE SW3
TEL 020 7589 5171
www.capitalhotel.co.uk
Classic English fabrics and antiques decorate this design-conscious yet conservative and immaculate hotel that has both rooms and apartments. Its restaurant serves fine British-inspired cuisine.

(i) 49 🚇 *Knightsbridge*

■ The Goring
£££££
BEESTON PLACE
GROSVENOR GARDENS SW1
TEL 020 7396 9000
thegoring.com
Run by the Goring family since 1910, this hotel promises top-notch hospitality and service, and each room is individually designed and decorated. The excellent restaurant serves both traditional and contemporary British cuisine. The clublike bar is also first-rate and has an impressive list of Champagnes.

(i) 71 🚇 *Victoria*

■ The Halkin
£££££
HALKIN STREET SW1
TEL 020 7333 1000
comohotels.com
This fashion-conscious hotel's

TRAVEL ESSENTIALS

decoration is inspired by classic Italian style—notably the sleek design, excellent air-conditioning and lighting control, and staff dressed in Armani. Elena Arzak is the chef behind the Ametsa Basque restaurant.

ⓘ 41 🏨 Hyde Park Corner

■ Jumeirah Carlton Tower
£££££
CADOGAN PLACE SW1
TEL 020 7235 1234
jumeirah.com
An impressive modern hotel, whose sky-high swimming pool and health club indicate top-quality services at all levels; Chinoiserie lounge for tea, Rib Room Bar for traditional food. It underwent renovation in 2019–20, refreshing the hotel with sensational styling.

ⓘ 216 🏨 Knightsbridge

■ The Lanesborough
£££££
HYDE PARK CORNER SW1
TEL 020 7259 5599
lanesborough.com
Evoking classical elegance in Regency style, this hotel offers lavish furnishings and divinely comfortable rooms. Its Céleste restaurant is Michelin-starred, and afternoon teas are served. Vintage cognacs in the Library Bar and Withdrawing Room, Havanas in the Garden Room, and butler service available.

ⓘ 93 🏨 Hyde Park Corner

■ Mandarin Oriental Hyde Park
£££££
66 KNIGHTSBRIDGE SW1
TEL 020 7235 2000
mandarinoriental.com

A splendid Edwardian landmark, extravagantly and sumptuously refurbished in 2019. The large rooms (request a view of Hyde Park) have lavish bathrooms. Two outstanding restaurants are the French Bar Boulud, overseen by Daniel Boulud, and the first London venture from Britain's own three-Michelin-star chef, Heston Blumenthal, called Dinner by Heston Blumenthal.

ⓘ 181 🏨 Knightsbridge

■ The Knightsbridge
££££
10 BEAUFORT GARDENS SW3
TEL 020 7584 6300
firmdale.com
Situated in a good location for Knightsbridge shopping, with upscale rooms to match. No bar, restaurant, or gym, but a great room-service menu plus a cozy library-lounge.

ⓘ 44 🏨 Knightsbridge

■ The Rockwell
£££
181–183 CROMWELL ROAD SW5
TEL 020 7244 2000
therockwell.com
One of London's best recent openings occupies a listed historic building. Rooms are all different, though all share elegant and understated contemporary styling.

ⓘ 40 🏨 Earl's Court

■ B&B Belgravia
££
64–66 EBURY STREET SW1
TEL 020 7259 8570
bb-belgravia.com
Away from chintz and notably 21st century, this is freshness and contemporary quality introducing a new

understanding of a "B&B," from quality bed linen and power showers to really good breakfasts.

ⓘ 17 🏨 Victoria

EAST LONDON
The revitalization of East London has transformed it into one of the coolest parts of the city, with a lively arts scene and street markets.

■ Canary Riverside Plaza
£££££
46 WESTFERRY CIRCUS E14
TEL 020 7510 1999
canaryriversideplaza.com
Canary Wharf's first deluxe hotel pampers guests with airy rooms (many with river views), plus all modern conveniences including a spa, large pool overlooking the river, and tennis courts.

ⓘ 142 🏨 Canary Wharf

■ The Zetter Hotel
££££
86–88 CLERKENWELL ROAD EC1
TEL 020 7324 4567
thezetter.com
This cool loft-hotel, in a restored 19th-century warehouse, is decorated with 1970s' furniture, old books, and modern technology

ⓘ 59 🏨 Farringdon

■ The Hoxton
£££
81 GREAT EASTERN STREET EC2
TEL 020 7550 1000
hoxtonhotels.com
One of London's trendiest neighborhoods has one of its trendiest hotels, decorated with work from local artists.

ⓘ 205 🏨 Shoreditch High Street

INDEX

CREDITS

Walking London
Sara Calian

Since 1888, the National Geographic Society has funded more than 14,000 research, exploration, and preservation projects around the world. National Geographic Partners distributes a portion of the funds it receives from your purchase to National Geographic Society to support programs including the conservation of animals and their habitats.

National Geographic Partners, LLC
1145 17th Street NW
Washington, DC 20036-4688 USA

Get closer to National Geographic explorers and photographers, and connect with our global community. Join us today at nationalgeographic.org/joinus

For rights or permissions inquiries, please contact National Geographic Books Subsidiary Rights: bookrights@natgeo.com

Edition edited by White Star s.r.l.
Licensee of National Geographic Partners, LLC.
Update by Christopher P. Baker

The information in this book has been carefully checked and to the best of our knowledge is accurate. However, details are subject to change, and the publisher cannot be responsible for such changes, or for errors or omissions. Assessments of sites, hotels, and restaurants are based on the author's subjective opinions, which do not necessarily reflect the publisher's opinion.

ISBN: 978-88-544-1587-4

Printed in China
23/TL/2

MIX
Paper from
responsible sources
FSC® C178000
FSC www.fsc.org

CREDITS